IF I CAN
YOU CAN
LEARN
ENGLISH
TOO!

Mohammed Wasim

PARTRIDGE

A Penguin Random House Company

To order additional copies of this book, contact
Partridge India
000 800 10062 62
orders.india@partridgepublishing.com

www.partridgepublishing.com/india

Dedication

*F*irst of all I would like to thank my personal saviour Lord Jesus Christ. Only in Him is the salvation. I am very much thankful to Rev Dong Wook Cho. Without his sponsorship I couldn't move forward to publish this book. I am very much grateful to his kind consideration and converting my dream into reality. Henceforth he is my great mentor and influencer. He always guides to my dream and thought; he optimizes me bit by bit.

This book is dedicated to a very special person of my life Rev Purna Bahadur Chettri. He is my God father and every means of my life. What I'm now is because of him. He has an immense contribution over my career and life. Eventually I would like to dedicate this book to all those people without whom this book would not have been possible. My very special and sincere thanks to those who spent their valuable times on my manuscript and defined my venture more optimistically and of course my Daughter's influence (Ms Afizah Alexander Wasim). She is an angel for me and very precious gift of my life.

Learning is the subway to have an incredible knowledge. So keep on learning.

Learning is the freedom of your insights. So keep on discovering.

I highly recommend this book by Mr. Mohammed Wasim for anyone who desires a high command of English.

The vocabularies and expressions covered in the book are those which are often used incorrectly in both spoken and written English.

I strongly believe that the alphabetized lexicon at the end of the book will be found useful by numerous readers.

Dr. Seung Soo Kim
(He is retired professor of department of English Literature in JeonJu University, in South Korea.)

Among a plenty of reference books regard to English, this book brings you the enhancement of a life on English. It is the eyes-open book which makes you to mine out the hidden treasures of English which already you have potentially through easy and systematic approach.

Dr. David W Cho
(The Principal, All Nations Theological Seminary. India)

Greetings! I went through the draft which has a great potential. With my little over 5 years of experience of copy editing, proof reading and publication of ISSN/ISBN Journals & Books, I can say this for sure that to make a book publish is like gestating a child for 9 months, go through the pain of labour and give birth. But soon after the birth—the book will bring smile to many. I wish that your book will be really purposeful.

Peter Lepcha,
Assistant Professor (Former Head), Department of English
Campus Co-ordinator & Public Information Officer (PIO)
Salesian College Siliguri

This book will be useful both for the learner as well as the learned. Since the book contains the useful words arranged alphabetically it will be easier for the reader and the learner to find out the words required for his purpose. The book contains the meaning of the word with the practical use of the word which makes a user easy to locate the word according to his needs. The compiler has so meticulously compiled this book that it would be a guide book for all works of life.

Denis Lepcha M.A. B.Ed. M.Phil (Diploma Hons in Classical Philosophy and Education). St. Robert's High School Darjeeling.
Assistant teacher St. Robert's high school Darjeeling. Freelance writer in Nepali daily. Resource person family commission Roman Catholic diocese of Darjeeling. general secretary indigenous Lepcha tribal association.

CHAPTER 1

One Word Substitution Errors

To make one's writing tense, economical and persuasive, one should have a good knowledge of One Word Substitutes. They can serve the purpose of many words. They make language clear, colourful and economical. But we are likely to make errors in their use because of lack of their proper sense and form.

Few examples are given in the following:

1) **Atheist**
a) A person who loves mankind.
   A person who does not believe in God.

2) **Acquaint**.
a) To be free from a charge.
b) To be familiar with a person and thing.

3) **Adolescence.**
a) Ignorance of a matter.
b) Age between boyhood and youth.

4) **Amateur**
a) Something done as a hobby.
b) A person not mature.

5) **Autobiography**
a) A life-story by the person himself.
b) An automatic machine.

6) **Automobile**
a) A self-dependent person.
b) Vehicles which move automatically.

7) **Amnesty**
a) The sense of honesty and justice.
b) An act of pardonning in general.

8) **Amphibian**
a) One that can live both in water and on land alike.
b) Water-born disease.

9) **Bibliophile**
a) A list of books etc.
b) One who loves books.

10) **Bibliography**
a) A list of books and subjects.
b) A catalogue of famous persons.

11) **Biped**
a) An animal with two feet
b) A reptile.

12) **Celibacy**
a) A state of being unmarried.
b) A state of being ill.

13) **Centenary**
a) A creature having hundred feet
b) A span of hundred years.

14) **Contemporaries**
a) People living at the same period
b) People condemned

15) **Carnivorous**
a) Animal feeding on vegetables.
b) Animal feeding on flesh.

16) **Dessert**
a) A barren land
b) Sweet course

17) **Declamation**
a) Art of rhetorical exercise.
b) To say something by shouting.

18) **Dieting**
a) Fasting on religious grounds.
b) Small allowance of food to become slim.

19) **Egoist**
a) A person who treats self-interest everywhere.
b) One who is soul-conscious.

20) **Epitaph**
a) Short narrative poem.
b) Writing on a tomb.

21) **Epicure**
a) One who is choosy in eating and drinking.
b) A cure for many diseases.

22) **Epistle**
a) A kind of pistol.
b) Verse in form of a letter.

23) **Etiquette**
a) Set manner of conduct.
b) Immoral conduct.

24) **Fastidious**
a) One not easily pleased.
b) A corrupt person.

25) **Fatal**
a) Something resulting in death.
b) Something related to fate.

26) **Galaxy**
a) A shining object.
b) Luminous band of stars.

27) **Gazette**
a) A device or machine etc.
b) A government publication relating to orders, no tification, etc.

28) **Glossary**
a) A long list of books and magazine.
b) A long list of words and meanings.

29) **Hearse**
a)   A carriage drawn by a horse.
b)   Carriage to carry dead person.

30) **Heritage**
a)   Personal property and wealth.
b)   What is got from ancestors.

31) **Incredible**
a)   Which cannot be believed.
b)   Which brings fame and credit.

32) **Illiterate**
a)   A person who cannot read or write.
b)   An educated person.

33) **Illusion**
a)   False perception.
b)   A thing scene in a dream.

34) **Juvenile**
a)   Relating to young and the youth.
b)   Not ripe and mature.

35) **Lunar**
a)   Of love and marriage.
b)   Something relating to moon.

36) **Manuscript**
a)   Script for a film.
b)   A book etc. written by hand.

37) **Muse**
a) To enjoy something.
b) To goddess of arts.

38) **Name-sake**
a) An assumed and false name.
b) Having the same name as the other.

39) **Omniscient**
a) Present everywhere.
b) Knowing all and everything.

40) **Obesity**
a) Having a lot of fat in one's body.
b) Capacity to work hard.

41) **Orphan**
a) A person without father and mother.
b) A homeless person.

42) **Obituary**
a) A notice of death in a newspaper.
b) A place where birds are kept.

43) **Pastoral**
a) Literature of shepherds and pasture.
b) A disease relating to virus.

44) **Philanthropist**
a) One who leads a luxurious life.
b) One who loves and works for mankind.

45) **Prejudice**
a)   To have a baseless opinion against anybody.
b)   Hostile with a person.

46) **Quack**
a)   The cry of a duck
b)   One who pretends skill in medicine and surgery.

47) **Questionnaire**
a)   An interrogative sentence.
b)   Formulated series of questions.

48) **Red-tapism**
a)   Too much of official formality.
b)   Too dangerous to undertake.

49) **Referendum**
a)   To refer a case to higher authority.
b)   Decision by general vote on a single questions.

50) **Robot**
a)   A very healthy and wise person.
b)   An intelligent and obedient man like machine.

51) **Sanatorium**
a)   A temple of the Jews.
b)   A place of good climate where invalids are kept.

52) **Spectrum**
a)   A beautiful sight full of colours.
b)   Image formed by rays of light.

53) **Secular**
a) That does not favour any religion.
b) Something irreligious.

54) **Teetotallar**
a) One who dislikes tea etc.
b) One who abstains from intoxicating drinks.

55) **Terminus**
a) A term examination.
b) Station at the end of route.

56) **Ubiquitous**
a) Quarrelsome.
b) Found or present everywhere.

57) **Vertebrate**
a) Animals having spinal column.
b) Animals living on land only.

58) **Veteran**
a) An aged person.
b) A person having long experience of an occupation etc.

59) **Weather-cock**.
a) An unreliable person.
b) A device to show the direction of air.

60) **Zodiac**
a) A belt of heavenly bodies into twelve equal parts.
b) A disease of the skin.

CHAPTER 2

How To Handle Homonyms

A homonyms is a word with almost the same pronunciation as another, but with a different meaning. Theses homonyms go in pairs and cause many errors and confusion in writing to unwary writers. They use erroneously one for another for they do not know the exact meaning of the pairs of words. The words being similar in sound and pronunciation perplex the students a lot. They are so deceptive as appear synonyms. They pose a great difficulty and a pitfall.

Below the uses of wrong words instead of the correct one.

1) He willingly **EXCEPTED** my invitation. (incorrect)
   He willingly **ACCEPTED** my invitation. (correct)

2) My father gave me a good piece of **ADVISE**.
   My father gave me a good piece of **ADVICE**.

3) Overwork **EFFECTED** her health.
   Overwork **AFFECTED** her health.

4) Dr. Afizah has been a famous **ANUALIST**.
   Dr. Afizah has been a famous **ANNUALIST**.

5) His lecture was full of **ANTEDOTES**.
   His lecture was full of **ANCEDOTES**.

6) Convey my best **COMPLEMENTS** to your parents.
   Convey my best **COMPLIMENTS** to your parents.

7) He is an employee of Delhi Municipal
   COOPERATION.
   He is an employee of Delhi Municipal
   CORPORATION.

8) Your signature on the **CHECK** did not tally.
   Your signature on the **CHEQUE** did not tally.

9) I was pained by his **DEPRECITORY** remarks.
   I was pained by his **DEPRECATORY** remarks.

10) The camel is the ship of the **DESSERT**.
    The camel is the ship of the **DESERT**.

11) I got up from my chair in **DIFFERENCE.**
    I got up from my chair in **DEFERENCE.**

12) Why did you **DEIFY** the orders of your boss?
    Why did you **DEFY** the orders of your boss?

13) Their relation is **ELICIT**.
    Their relation is **ILLICIT**.

14) John Spanring was an **IMMINENT** novelist.
    John Spanring was an **EMINENT** novelist.

15) **ACCESS** of everything is bad.
    EXCESS of everything is bad.

16) Where is your **FARE** copy?
    Where is your **FAIR** copy?

17) He added **FARTHER**.
    He added **FURTHER**.

18) I recognized him from his **GATE**.
    I recognized him from his **GAIT**.

19) Gandhiji was **HOLY** devoted to human welfare.
    Gndhiji was **WHOLLY** devoted to human welfare.

20) He has **LOSE** morals.
    He has **LOOSE** morals.

21) He is man of **PRINCIPALS.**
    He is man of **PRINCIPLES**.

22) Go and see him in the **PERSONAL** department.
    Go and see him in the **PERSONNEL** department.

23) I want to get a **BIRTH** reserved for my father.
    I want to get a **BERTH** reserved for my father.

24) What is the **ROUTH** cause of corruption?
    What is the **ROOT** cause of corruption?

25) **THERE** house is large and beautiful.
    THEIR house is large and beautiful.

26) This news is **TO** good **TOO** be true.
    This news is **TOO** good **TO** be true.

27) **FORMALLY** he was our principal.
    FORMERLY he was our principal.

28) A hermit **LEAVED** in a hut.
    A hermit **LIVED** in a hut.

29) **RIGHTS** and rituals are part of religious life.
    RITES and rituals are part of religious life.

30) You have **SUFFICIENT** sense to know better.
    You have **ENOUGH** sense to know better.

CHAPTER 3

AUXILIARIES AMISS

An auxiliary verb is a word (verb) that helps to form tenses, moods or voices of other verbs. There are some auxiliaries like, **will, shall, may, ought** etc. which are quite confusion. It is necessary that we are familiar with their current uses.

Will and **Shall** are used to form the simple future. Shall is used in the first person, that is, with I and we to show the future of the verb. Will is used with the second and third persons. But when their use is reversed they show determination, command or person.

Would and **Should** are past tense of will and shall. Should is used to denote surprise, duty, obligations, supposition, condition and future in the past. Would is used to express request, desire, past habit willingness, determination unreal condition, etc.

May is used to indicate purpose, permission, possibility and desire. **Might**, the past tense of may, denotes possibility but then there is an element of doubt. Might also expresses politeness, suggestion, purpose and desire.

A few scrolls at the bottom:

1) <u>CAN</u> I come in, Sir? (incorrect)
   (Permission)
   <u>MAY</u> I come in, Sir? (correct)

2) They <u>SHALL</u> go and work there.
   (Simple Future)
   They <u>WILL</u> go and work there.

3) I <u>WILL</u> take you to the doctor.
   (Simple Future)
   I <u>SHALL</u> take you to the doctor.

4) You <u>WILL</u> neither kill nor harm.
   (Command)
   You <u>SHALL</u> neither kill nor harm.

5) We <u>SHALL</u> meet you positively.
   (Promise)
   We <u>WILL</u> meet you positively.

6) We <u>SHALL</u> fight hard and defeat the enemy.
   (Determination)
   We <u>WILL</u> Fight Hard and defeat the enemy.

7) I <u>SHALL</u> lend the money you need.
   (Willingness)
   I <u>WILL</u> lend the money you need.

8) I <u>AM</u> sure he <u>SHALL</u> forgive you.
   (Promise)
   I <u>AM</u> sure he <u>WILL</u> forgive you.

9) You <u>WILL</u> pay dearly for the lapse.
    (Threat)
    You <u>SHALL</u> pay dearly for the lapse.

10) <u>CAN</u> I come and see you to next day?
    (Permission)
    <u>MAY</u> I come and see you to next day?

11) You <u>WILL</u> stay till evening.
    (Command)
    You <u>SHALL</u> stay till evening.

12) I <u>MAY</u> lift a weight of 120 kgs.
    (Ability)
    I <u>CAN</u> lift a weight of 120 kgs.

13) For how long you <u>MAY</u> stand on your head?
    (Ability)
    For how long you <u>CAN</u> stand on you head?

14) It <u>CAN</u> do you much good.
    (Possibility)
    It <u>MAY</u> do you much good.

15) <u>MIGHT</u> you have a long life.
    (Wish)
    <u>MAY</u> you have a long life.

16) <u>MIGHT</u> we live to see the 21st century?
    (Desire)
    <u>MAY</u> we live to see the 21st century?

17) I would do it if I <u>CAN.</u>
(Possibility)
I would do it if I <u>COULD</u>.

18) I <u>SHALL</u> have seen him if he had been in the town.
(Possibility)
I <u>SHOULD</u> have seen him if he had been in the town.

19) <u>SHOULD</u> you like to have a cup of tea?
(Politeness)
<u>WOULD</u> you like to have a cup of tea?

20) <u>WOULD</u> I carry your box for you?
(Politeness)
<u>SHOULD</u> I carry your box for you?

21) It is strange that you <u>WOULD</u> fail.
(Surprise)
It is strange that you <u>SHOULD</u> fail.

22) Laxmi <u>SHOULD</u> sit and work all day.
(Habit)
Laxmi <u>WOULD</u> sit and work all day.

23) We thought that it <u>MAY</u> rain.
(Guess)
We thought it <u>MIGHT</u> rain.

24) You <u>SHOULD</u> perform your duty.
(FORCE)
You <u>MUST</u> perform your duty.

25) I <u>SHOULD</u> buy the book because the bookseller has kept it for me.
(Obligation)
I <u>OUGHT</u> to buy the book because the bookseller has kept it for me.

26) You <u>SHOULD NOT</u> know **Hindi** to travel in India.
(Suggestion)
You N<u>EED NOT </u>know **HINDI** to travel in India.

CHAPTER 4

Sequential Lapses

Sequence means succession or continuity. In other words the sequence is the principle according to which a sentence follows another within a long sentence. Many errors are committed in spoken and written English because of the lack of proper relationship in sequence of tenses. The rule is that the verb of the principal clause is followed by the verb in subordinate clause in relation to time. A verb in past tense in the main clause is invariably followed by a verb in the subordinate clause.

The reader is advised to go carefully through the following sentences.

1) He knew that the bridge **IS** not safe. (incorrect)
    He knew that the bridges **WAS** not safe. (correct)

2) He sent for the doctor because I **AM** ill.
    He sent for the doctor because I **WAS** ill.

3) The inspector wanted to know why I **HAVE** no driving licence.
    The inspector wanted to know why I **HAD** no driving licence.

4) I saw that I **MAKE** a mistake.
   I saw that I **MADE** a mistake.

5) He walked so fast that no other person **CAN** keep pace with him.
   He walked so fast that no other person **COULD** keep pace with him.

6) I studied hard that I **MAY** get first class.
   I studied hard that I **MIGHT** get first class.

7) Do you know who discovered that the earth **MOVED** round the sun?
   Do you know who discovered that the earth **MOVES** round the sun?

8) He said that truth ultimately **TRIUMPHED**.
   He said that truth ultimately **TRIUMPHS**.

9) I asked him if Rajesh **HAS** come.
   I asked him if Rajesh **HAD** come.

10) Rima told me you **WILL** accompany her.
    Rima told me you **WOULD** accompany her.

11) I never thought that **SHALL** see you again.
    I never thought that I **SHOULD** see you again.

12) He said that he **WANTS** more money.
    He said that he **WANTED** more money.

13) We waited till the rain **STOPS**.
    We waited till the rain **STOPPED**.

14) Wherever he preached, people **FLOCK** in large number.
Wherever he preached, people **FLOCK** in large number.

15) The patient told the doctor that he **FEELS** better.
The patient told the doctor that he **FELT** better.

16) He gave me more than he **GAVE** to my brother.
He gave me more than he **IS GIVING** to my brother.

CHAPTER 5

Why Adverbs Go Wrong

Adverbs often confuse us because we fail to distinguish them from adjectives, most of the adverbs end in **ly,** but not always. In latters condition one may find oneself in trouble. Adverbs are **when**, **where** and **how** words. They modify a verb, an adjective or another adverb. An adverb attends upon a verb as does an adjective upon a noun. Sometimes it is not easy to use adverbs correctly, and so they go awry making our sentences incorrect. Study the following sentences.

1) I <u>CANNOT SCARECLY</u> ignore his views. (incorrect)
   I <u>CAN SACRCELY</u> ignore his views. (correct)

2) He stood first because he <u>WORKS HARDLY</u>.
   He stood first because he <u>WORKED HARD</u>.

3) He speaks <u>FLUENT</u> than I.
   He speaks <u>FLUENTLY</u> than I.

4) Don't you feel <u>GOOD</u> now?
   Don't you feel <u>WELL</u> now?

5) She <u>MOSTLY</u> touched the line.
   She <u>ALMOST</u> touched the line.

6) He had hardly reached the bus-stop <u>THAN</u> the bus left.
    He had hardly reached the bus-stop <u>WHEN</u> the bus left.

7) Never think <u>BAD</u> of anyone.
    Never think <u>ILL</u> of anyone.

8) They were treated <u>ROYAL</u>.
    They were treated <u>ROYALLY</u>.

9) The oranges taste <u>SOURELY</u>.
    The oranges taste <u>SOUR</u>.

10) I never expected that he would treat you so <u>ROUGH</u>.
    I never expected that he would treat you so <u>ROUGHLY</u>.

11) He has <u>RETURNED BACK</u> from London.
    He has <u>RETURNED</u> from London.

12) <u>SOMETIME</u> it so happens.
    <u>SOMETIMES</u> it so happens.

13) I <u>CANNOT BARELY</u> see it now.
    I <u>CAN BARELY</u> see it now.

14) They reside <u>BESIDES</u> the college.
    They reside <u>BESIDE</u> the college.

15) <u>DESPITE</u> of his hard work he is poor.
    <u>DESPITE</u> his hard work he is poor.

16) When did you <u>COME CROSS</u> my friend?
    When did you <u>COME ACROSS</u> my friend?

17) I searched my purse but could not find it
    <u>NOWHERE</u>.
    I searched my purse but could not find it
    <u>ANYWHERE</u>.

18) I was <u>NEVER BORN</u> in London.
    I was <u>NOT BORN</u> in London.

19) I <u>NEVER</u> remember having seen you.
    I <u>DON'T</u> remember having seen you.

20) Sing <u>LOWLY</u> but <u>CLEARLY</u>.
    Sing <u>LOW</u> but <u>CLEAR</u>.

21) Early you come, the <u>GOOD</u>,
    Early you come, the <u>BETTER</u>.

22) This diamond is <u>EQUALLY AS VALUABLE AS</u> that.
    This diamond <u>AS VALUABLE AS</u> that.

23) The Ganga <u>DESCENDS</u> down to the plains at
    Rishikesh.
    The Ganga <u>DECENDS</u> to the plains of Rishikesh.

24) <u>REPEAT AGAIN</u> what you have said.
    <u>REPEAT</u> what you have said.

25) Your food is <u>EQUALLY AS GOOD AS</u> mine.
    Your food is <u>AS GOOD AS</u> mine.

CHAPTER 6

Errors In The Use Of Adjectives

Adjectives are words which tell us something about other words, that is, nouns. It is not possible to speak or write without the use of adjectives. We add colour, beauty and meaning to the nouns by using adjectives. We speak of an ideal teacher, sweet face, blue eyes, dark Complexion, worst situation, etc. We commit errors in the use of adjectives because we either confuse them with the adverbs or the nouns.

The basic difference between adjectives and adverbs should always be kept in mind. While comparing two persons or things the comparative degree is used. When comparison involves more, than two persons or things, the superlative degree is used. Generally adjectives of one syllable form their comparative and superlative degrees by adding -**er** and -**est** respectively to them. But some adjectives are more like irregular verbs and they should be learnt.

Follow:

1) He has been suffering from a <u>CHRONICLE</u> disease. (incorrect)
    He has been suffering from a <u>CHRONIC</u> disease. (correct)

2) I don't feel <u>FINELY</u>.
I don't feel <u>FINE</u>.

3) Give me a piece of <u>COURSE</u> cloth.
Give me a piece of <u>COARSE</u> cloth.

4) He came to the office as <u>USUALLY</u>.
He came to the office as <u>USUAL</u>.

5) <u>ANY</u> men were present at the meeting.
<u>SOME</u> men were present at the meeting.

6) Many a <u>STUDENTS ARE</u> industrious.
Many a <u>STUDENT IS</u> industrious.

7) <u>A LITTLE</u> persons donated their blood.
<u>A FEW</u> persons donated their blood.

8) <u>LITTLE</u> information I could get was not enough.
<u>THE LITTLE</u> information I could get was not enough.

9) No <u>LESS</u> than 40 persons came.
No <u>FEWER</u> than 40 persons came.

10) <u>A SEVERAL</u> men and women visited the fair.
<u>SEVERAL</u> men and women visited the fair.

11) <u>ANY</u> dozen articles were broken.
<u>SOME</u> dozen articles were broken.

12) We needed <u>FEW</u> rain, but <u>ANY</u> more sunshine.
We needed <u>LESS</u> rain, but <u>MUCH</u> more sunshine.

13) I want <u>LITTLE</u> milk.
I want <u>SOME</u> milk.

14) Don't talk <u>MUCH</u> nonsense.
Don't talk <u>SUCH</u> nonsense.

15) <u>LITTLE</u> persons talk of great.
<u>SMALL</u> persons talk of great.

16) These mangoes taste so <u>DELICIOUSLY</u>.
These mangoes taste so <u>DELICIOUS</u>.

17) Of the two evils, choose the <u>LEAST</u> one.
Of the two evils, choose the <u>LESSER</u> one.

18) He gave me a <u>PARTIENTLY</u> hearing.
He gave me a <u>PATIENT</u> hearing.

19) My brother is elder <u>THAN I AM</u>.
My brother is elder <u>TO ME</u>.

20) This is the <u>ELDEST</u> temple.
This is the <u>OLDEST</u> temple.

21) Is he your <u>OLDER</u> brother?
Is he your <u>ELDER</u> brother?

22) The <u>MUCH</u> you work the <u>GOOD</u> you are.
The <u>MORE</u> you work the <u>BETTER</u> you are.

23) He is the tallest man <u>THAN</u> all.
He is the tallest man <u>OF</u> all.

24) He was <u>DEARER</u> of all the sons.
He was <u>THE DEAREST</u> of all the sons.

25) I have never seen a <u>MORE WORSE</u> situation than this.
I have never seen <u>WORSE</u> situation than this.

26) The roses smell <u>MORE SWEETLY</u> in the morning.
The roses smell <u>MORE SWEET</u> in the morning.

27) <u>THESE KINDS</u> of mistake does occur.
<u>THIS KIND</u> of mistake does occur.

28) He is better educated than <u>ANOTHER</u> man.
He is better educated than <u>ANY OTHER</u> man.

29) This is the <u>LEAST</u> news I received.
This is the <u>LAST</u> news I received.

30) <u>THOSE</u> type of mango tastes sweet.
<u>THAT</u> type of mango tastes sweet.

31) I am not as <u>TALLER</u> as you.
I am not as <u>TALL</u> as you.

32) Mauritius is a <u>WORTH SEEING PLACE</u>.
Mauritius is a <u>PLACE WORTH SEEING</u>.

33) I want my <u>PRINCIPAL</u> amount.
I want my <u>PRINCIPEL</u> amount.

34) The more the <u>MERRIEST</u>.
The more the <u>MERRIER.</u>

35) Gorden and John are brothers. Gorden is older
THAN LATER.
Gorden and John are brothers. Gorden is older TO
FORMER.

36) RICH should help POOR.
THE RICH should help THE POOR.

37) Open your book at FORTY PAGE.
Open your book at PAGE FORTY.

38) WHOLE town was excited.
THE WHOLE town was excited.

39) Gold is PRECIOUS than any metal.
Gold is MORE PRECIOUS than any metal.

CHAPTER 7

Pitfalls Of Plurality

There are two numbers in English, singular and plural. The former denotes one person or thing, the latter more than one person or thing. Most of the nouns form their plurals by addition of **"s"** or **"es"**. Nouns ending with **"y"** preceded by a consonant form their plurals by changing **"y"** but preceded by a vowel take **"s"** for their plurals.

Nouns ending with "o" preceded by a consonant, form their plurals by adding **"es"**. Those ending with **"oo"**, **"io"** and **"yo"** preceded by a consonant add **"s"** to form plurals. But there are some **"o"** ending nouns which take **"s"** or **"es"** for their plurals.

Some nouns ending with **"f"** or **"fe"** form their plurals by changing **"f"** or **"fe"** into **"ves"**, but a few such nouns add only **"s"** to change into plurals.

Below is given a list of common errors in regard to the plurals.

1) There grew a clamp of **BAMBOOES**. (incorrect)
    There grew a clamp of **BAMBOOS**. (correct)

2) He ran after the two **THIEFS** and caught one.
   He ran after the two **THIEVES** and caught one.

3) There are four **SHELFS** in my almirah.
   There are four **SHELVES** in my almirah.

4) All the **MOTHER-IN-LAWS** of the colony
   assembled into a meeting.
   All the **MOTHERS-IN-LAW** of the colony
   assembled into a meeting.

5) He is one of the **COMMANDER-IN-CHIEFS**.
   He is one of the **COMMANDERS-IN-CHIEF**.

6) One of the **PASSER-BYS** rescued her.
   One of the **PASSERS-BY** rescued her.

7) Dot your **IS** and cross your **TS**.
   Dot your **I'S** and cross your **T'S**.

8) They were all **MISSS**.
   They were all **MISSES**.

9) My junior and senior **MASTER'S** have come.
   My junior and senior **MASTERS** have come.

10) Both his **FOOTS** got injured.
    Both his **FEET** got injured.

11) There were a number of **MOUSES**.
    There were a number of **MICE**.

12) Have you gone through the **PROOVES** of the book?
Have you gone through the **PROOFS** of the book?

13) I bought two pairs of **OXES**.
I bought two pairs of **OXEN**.

14) A cat is said to have nine **LIFES**.
A cat is said to have nine **LIVES**.

15) The members of the same community are called **BROTHERS**.
The members of the same community are called **BRETHERN**.

16) What are the **CRITERION**?
What are the **CRITERIA**?

17) Don't call them **SWINES**.
Don't call them **SWINE**.

18) **HOUSEFLYS** carry diseases.
HOUSEFLIES carry diseases.

19) He has started giving himself **AIR**.
He has started giving himself **AIRS**.

20) Give the beggar two **LOAFS** of bread.
Give the beggar two **LOAVES** of bread.

21) Who has broken my **SCISSOR**?
Who has broken my **SCISSOR**?

22) **LADYS** and **GENTELMENS**.
LADIES and **GENTELMEN**.

23) I have misplaced my **SPECTACLE**.
I have misplaced my **SPECTACLES**.

24) He deals in **CURIOS**.
He deals in **CURIOS**.

25) What are the **BASISES** of your allegation?
What are the **BASES** of your allegation?

26) Many **BLIND-BELIEVES** prevail among them.
Many **BLIND-BELIEFS** prevail among them.

27) Six **THOUSANDS** rupees is a good amount.
Six **THOUSAND** rupees is a good amount.

28) **CATTLES** are grazing in the field.
CATTLE are grazing in the field.

29) He has given me **MANY** informations.
He has given me **MUCH** information.

30) With best **COMPLIMENT**.
With best **COMPLIMENTS**.

31) She is mother of three **CHILDS**.
She is mother of three **CHILDREN**.

32) We lived in spacious **PREMISE**.
We lived in spacious **PREMISES**.

33) I dislike your **BUTS AND IFS**.
    I dislike your **BUT'S AND IF'S**.

34) This movie is full of **NONSENSES**.
    This movie is full of **NONSENSE**.

35) **RICH** is earned by hardwork.
    RICHES is earned by hardwork.

CHAPTER 8

Awkward Use Of Articles

"A" or **"an"** are indefinite articles. **"A"** is used before a word beginning with a consonant, or a sound like a consonant. **"An"** is used before words beginning with a vowel or words beginning with a mute **"h"**.

"The" is the definite article. It is used for singular and plural and all genders. It is used before nouns of which there is only one, that is, the earth, the sky etc. it is used before a common noun denoting a class.

"The" is used in the comparative degree when selection is expressed. It is also used in the superlative degree. Again it is used before a noun made definite. It is used before an adjective used to represent a class of persons. It is also used before names of seas, rivers etc. it is not used before proper nouns and abstract nouns.

The use of articles is not always easy. They often create confusion if one is not particular about them. Study the following sentences.

1) There are **A APPLE** and **A ORANGE**. (incorrect)
    There are **AN APPLE** and **AN ORANGE.** (correct)

2) They had **WIFE** among five of them.
They had **A WIFE** among five of them.

3) **MAYOR** inaugurated the fair.
THE MAYOR inaugurated the fair.

4) Wrap it in **A** envelope.
Wrap it in **AN** envelope.

5) I have **LOT** of work to do.
I have **A LOT** of work to do.

6) **HIMALAYAS** means an abode of snow.
THE HIMALAYAS means an abode of snow.

7) Please give **PIECE** of paper.
Please give **A PIECE** of paper.

8) Bring **BOOK AND PEN.**
Bring **A BOOK AND A PEN.**

9) He lives in **U. S. A.**
He lives in **THE U. S. A.**

10) He was made **HONORARY** member.
He was made **AN HONORARY** member.

11) He was **A** honest person.
He was **AN** honest person.

12) I have **BIBLE** and **QURAN.**
I have **THE BIBLE** and **THE QURAN.**

13) He was **A** one-eyed person.
He was **AN** one-eyed person.

14) **MORE** the better.
THE MORE the better.

15) **MORE** you study **BETTER** you achieve.
THE MORE you study **THE BETTER** you achieve.

16) Wanted **A** M. A. in English.
Wanted **AN** M. A. in English.

17) We stayed at **AN** hotel in Goa.
We stay at **A** hotel in Goa.

18) I am optimistic as regards **FURTHER** course.
I am optimistic as regards **THE FURTHER** course.

19) **THE MAN** is a social animal.
MAN is a social animal.

20) **THE TOKYO** is the Capital of Japan.
TOKYO is the Capital of Japan.

21) We are studying **THE ENGLISH**.
We are studying **ENGLISH**.

22) Mr Pranab Mukerjee is now **PRESIDENT** of India.
Mr Pranab Mukerjee is now **THE PRESIDENT** of India.

23) I bought mangoes by **DOZEN**.
I bought mangoes by **THE DOZEN**.

24) **THE BOTH** sisters were good actresses.
BOTHE THE sisters were good actresses.

25) Kalidas is called as **SHAKESPEARE** of India.
Kalidas is called as **THE SHAKESPEARE** of India.

26) Where there is **LIFE** there is hope.
Where there is **A LIFE** there is hope.

27) You owe me **A** thousand one hundred and one dollar.
You owe me **ONE** thousand one hundred and one dollar.

28) A letter brings **SUB-CONSCIOUS** to the forefront.
A letter brings **THE SUB-CONSCIOUS** to the forefront.

29) **TRADITION** of Christmas celebration is very old.
THE TRADITION of Christmas celebration is very old.

30) It is **A** interest novel.
It is **AN** interesting novel.

CHAPTER 9

Judicious Use Of Genders

There are two main genders in English. Masculine and Feminine. Many mistakes are made when one fails to make a judicious use of these two genders. The knowledge of other two genders: Neuter and Common is also found inadequate. Therefore, there is much confusion in regard to genders. Moon is feminine. And so are ships and trains, but the sun is masculine. Many masculine nouns form their feminine forms by adding **"ess"**, for example, actress, waitress, princess. Sometimes man or woman and male or female are placed before a noun to underline a particular sex. Study the following examples to avoid errors in the use of genders.

1) A <u>WOMAN-BEAR</u> attacked a hunter. (incorrect)
   A <u>SHE-BEAR</u> attacked a hunter. (correct)

2) A <u>MALE-SPARROW</u> got hurt with a running fan.
   A <u>COCK-SPARROW</u> got hurt with a running fan.

3) I have employed a <u>FEMALE-SERVANT</u>.
   I have employed a <u>MAID-SERVANT</u>.

4) She is still a <u>BACHELOR</u>.
   She is still a <u>SPINSTER</u>.

5) I caught a <u>MALE-FISH</u>.
   I caught a <u>MILTER</u>.

6) A <u>WOMAN-MURDERER</u> will be hanged tomorrow.
   A <u>MURDERESS</u> will be hanged tomorrow.

7) She proved a great <u>FEMAL-BENEFACTOR</u>.
   She proved a great <u>BENEFACTRESS</u>.

8) The village woman is said to be a <u>WIZARD</u>.
   The village woman is said to be a <u>WITCH</u>.

9) The MALE-COWS are used in drawing carts etc.
   The <u>OXEN</u> are used in drawing carts etc.

10) A <u>WOMAN-PRIEST</u> performed the rites.
    A <u>PRIESTESS</u> performed the rites.

11) An <u>ELEPHANTESS</u> was trumpeting.
    A <u>SHE ELEPHANT</u> was trumpeting.

12) She is a famous <u>POET</u>.
    She is a famous <u>POETESS</u>.

13) What is the name of the <u>LADY AUTHOR</u>?
    What is the name of the <u>AUTHORESS</u>?

14) She became <u>PATRON</u> of our association.
    She became <u>PATRONESS</u> of our association.

15) She wanted to become a <u>SHE-MONK</u>.
    She wanted to become a <u>NUN</u>.

16) She is my <u>LADY-NEPHEW</u>.
She is my <u>NIECE</u>.

17) The Duke came with his wife is <u>FEMALE-DUKE</u>.
The Duke came with his wife is <u>DUCHESS</u>.

18) The hunter killed a <u>FEMALE-PEACOCK</u>.
The hunter killed a <u>PEA-HEN</u>.

19) The lady disguised herself as a
<u>FEMALE-SHEPHERD</u>.
The lady disguised herself as a <u>SHEPHERDESS</u>.

20) What a <u>SHE-TEMPTER</u> she was!
What a <u>TEMPTRESS</u> she was!

CHAPTER 10

Puzzling Pronouns

Pronouns are the words used in place of nouns. Thus, they are substitute words. They save a lot of our time and make expression easy. A pronoun can be used as a subject, as an object and as a possessive. There is a lot of confusion in the use of theses three forms of pronouns. The use of personal pronouns like <u>who</u>, <u>when</u>, etc. further add to this confusion. They are also slippery and intriguing.

Always use the subjective form of pronoun as a subject of a verb an object of a verb or preposition. The possessive form should always be used to express possession.

The relative and interrogative pronoun **"who"** is subjective, and **"whom"** is objective. They used be used as such, but in informal speech and writing both are being used interchangeable.

1) I love my wife, do you love <u>YOUR'S</u>. (incorrect)
   I love my wife, do you love <u>YOURS</u>. (correct)

2) <u>HER</u> and <u>ME</u> were reading.
   <u>SHE</u> and <u>I</u> were reading.

3) <u>THEM</u> and I participated in the debate.
   <u>THEY</u> and I participated in the debate.

4) I and <u>MINE</u> wife were rewarded.
   I and <u>MY</u> wife were rewarded.

5) Let <u>WE</u> pledge.
   Let <u>US</u> pledge.

6) None of them <u>HAVE</u> paid their dues.
   None of them <u>HAS</u> paid their dues.

7) It was <u>ME</u> who landed him money.
   It was <u>I</u> who landed him money.

8) <u>OUR'S</u> is a reputed school.
   <u>OURS</u> is a reputed school.

9) One should do <u>HIS</u> duty well.
   One should do <u>ONE'S</u> duty well.

10) Each must contribute what <u>THEY</u> can.
    Each must contribute what <u>HE/ SHE</u> can.

11) This book is <u>MY</u> and that is <u>YOUR'S</u>.
    This book is <u>MINE</u> and that is <u>YOURS</u>.

12) <u>WHOM</u> do you think was there?
    <u>WHO</u> do you think was there?

13) <u>WHOM</u> do you expect will come first?
    <u>WHO</u> do you expect will come first?

14) <u>YOU</u>, <u>He</u> and <u>ME</u> will ever remain friends.
<u>YOU, HE</u> and <u>I</u> will ever remain friends.

15) <u>I, YOU</u> and <u>HE</u> worked in the same office.
<u>YOU, HE</u> and <u>I</u> worked in the same office.

16) Neither she nor they took <u>HER</u> money.
Neither she nor they took <u>THEIR</u> money.

17) <u>HER'S</u> was the choicest gift.
<u>HERS</u> was the choicest gift.

18) <u>HE</u> and <u>ME</u> are shareholders.
<u>HE</u> and <u>I</u> are shareholders.

19) Do you know <u>WHOM</u> they were?
Do you know <u>WHO</u> they were?

20) They are to blame <u>THEIRSELVES</u>.
They are to blame <u>THEMSELVES</u>.

21) <u>WHO</u> were you talking to?
<u>WHOM</u> were you talking to?

22) <u>WHO</u> did you see in the exhibition?
<u>WHOM</u> did you see in the exhibition?

23) Laxmi and Rima love <u>ONE ANOTHER</u>.
Laxmi and Rima love <u>EACH OTHER</u>.

24) What objection do you have to <u>I</u> going there?
What objection do you have to <u>MY</u> going there?

25) You can do as well as ME.
    You can do as well as I.

26) All was lost and nothing was left for you and I.
    All was lost and nothing was left for you and ME.

27) If anybody calls tell THEM I am not in town.
    If anybody calls tell HIM/ HER I am not in town.

28) I availed OF the opportunity.
    I availed MYSELF of the opportunity.

29) It is upto THEIRS to accept the offer.
    It is upto THEM to accept the offer.

30) WHO do you want to see now?
    WHOM do you want to see now?

CHAPTER 11

Tricky Participles

A participle is a verbal word having the qualities both of a verb and an adjective. Thus a participle combines both the nature of a verb and an adjective. Present participles end with **"ing"** and past participles **"en" "d"** with **"ed", "d", "t", "n" "or" "en"**. Confusion in the use of participles arises because they are left loose and dangling. Every participle should be supplied with the word that it modifies. Errors are there when participles are left unrelated or they are misplaced.

As a rule the participle as a modifier should be placed as close as possible to the word it modifies, so that their relationship is clearly seen. Thus, the modifiers should always have something to hang upon and not left unrelated and loose.

1) **BEING** Sunday, I did not go to office. (incorrect)
    IT BEING Sunday, I did not go to office. (correct)

2) **BEING** a short story, my friend came.
    WHILE I WAS REDAING a short story, my friend came.

3) **SLEEPING** in the courtyard, a thief entered the house.
   WHILE HE SLEPT IN the courtyard, a thief entered the house.

4) **COMING OUT**, he found his cycle there no more.
   AS HE CAME OUT, he found his cycle there no more.

5) Arriving in time on a cycle, **THE INAGURATION** of the function begin.
   Arriving in time on a cycle **I SAW THE INAUGURATION** of the function begin.

6) Reaching in time, **THE SHOW BEGAN**.
   Reaching in time, **I SAW THE SHOW BEGAN**.

7) **WINDING** the wrist watch, I saw her walking along the road.
   WHEN I WOUND the wrist watch, I saw her walking along the road.

8) **WATERING THE PLANTS** the clouds thundered.
   WHEN I WAS WATERING THE PLANTS, the clouds thundered.

9) **LYING** on the bed, the telephone rang.
   WHEN I LAY on the bed, the telephone rang.

10) **DEMONSTRATING**, a stick struck him.
    WHILE HE WAS DEMONSTRATING, a stick struck him.

CHAPTER 12

Contravention Of Conjunctions

The conjunctions are words which join words and sentences together. Thus, they make our speech and writing compact and precise. The conjunctions and the prepositions form the common links of English. They are both alike in function, but their basic difference lies in the fact that a conjunction connects words or sentences into a unit, while a preposition shows a relation of a noun or a pronoun with another word. A conjunction simply joints two elements and does no other function.

"Hardly" and "scarcely" are always followed by "when" and never by "than". "No sooner" is always followed by "than" and takes an interrogative verb in the main clause.

"Unless" means "if not" and so never takes not after it. "Lest" is followed by "should". It never takes "not" after it. "supposing" and "if" do not go together.

"until" and "unless" are negative and so are never followed by "not". "Though" and "although" always take "yet" after them. In the use of double conjunctions like either . . . . or neither . . . . .nor never use a positive with a negative.

Some nitty-gritty in the following:

1)   Neither a borrower **OR** a lender be. (incorrect)
     Neither a borrower **NOR** a lender be. (correct)

2)   Look sharp, **ELSE YOU WILL NOT** miss the train.
     Look sharp, **ELSE YOU WILL** miss the train.

3)   You must work hard **EITHER** you may fail.
     You must work hard **OR** you may fail.

4)   They were wounded, **BUT** they fought.
     They were wounded, **STILL** they fought.

5)   He was safe, **BUT** he was bruised.
     He was safe, **ONLY** he was bruised.

6)   Although it is raining, **BUT** I shall go.
     Although it is raining, **YET** I shall go.

7)   **FOR** when have you been in the city?
     SINCE when have you been in the city.

8)   He will not come **UNLESS YOU DON'T** insist.
     He will not come **UNLESS YOU** insist.

9)   Be careful lest **YOU DO NOT** fall ill.
     Be careful lest **YOU SHOULD** fall ill.

10) He was born to poor parents, **BUT** he covered
     himself with glory.
     He was born to poor parents, **NEVERTHLESS** he
     covered himself with glory.

11) **SCARCELY** had I entered the room **THAN** I saw her.
SCARCELY had I entered the room **WHEN** I saw her.

12) You would **SCARCELY** believe me **IF** I say I saw a ghost.
You would **SCARCELY** believe me **WHEN** I say I saw a ghost.

13) **NO SOONER** I reached the station **THE TRAIN** left.
NO SOONER DID I reach the station **THAN** the train left.

14) You can sing so well **LIKE** I can.
You can sing so well **AS** I can.

15) **ALTHOUGH** I am late, **BUT** I think I must start.
ALTHOUGH I am late, **YET** I think I must start.

16) **THOUGH** they tortured him, **BUT** he did not betray the trust.
THOUGH they tortured him, **YET** he did not betray the trust.

17) **UNTILL YOU DO NOT COME**, I shall be here.
UNTIL YOU COME, I shall be here.

18) Run fast **LEST YOU DO NOT MISS** the train.
Run fast **LEST YOU MISS** the train.

19) **SHE HAD** to accept all my terms or none at all.
EITHER **SH**E **HA**D to accept all my terms or none
at all.

20) He would **EITHER** starve than beg.
He would **RATHE**R starve than beg.

21) He has remained with us **TILL** he sold the flat.
He has remained with us **SINC**E he sold the flat.

22) Go **AT ONCE, YOU** would be punished.
Go **ONCE**, **OR YO**U would be punished.

23) I was **TOO GLAD** to meet my friend from Malickpur.
I was **VER**Y **GLA**D to meet my friend from
Malickpur.

24) He stood first **AND HE** got a prize.
He stood first **AN**D **THEREFOR**E go a prize.

25) I am wounded **AND** not defeated.
I am wounded **BU**T not defeated.

26) He is rich and generous **TO**.
He is rich and generous **TO**O.

27) He bought books, pen, papers **AND ETC**.
He bought books , pen, papers, **ET**C.

28) I have not even seen her **AND TALKED**.
I have not even seen her **LE**T **ALON**E **TALKIN**G.

29) He received me with open arms **AS** he saw me.
He received me with open arms **AS SOON AS** he saw me.

30) I **NOT ONLY ATE** biscuits, but also sweets.
I **ATE NOT ONLY** biscuits, but also sweets.

CHAPTER 13

COMPOUND COMPLICATIONS

A compound word is a combination of two or more word-elements, parts or ingredients. There are many colourful compounds. These should be carefully studied in order to use them correctly. Below are given a nice sampling of compound words which are likely to cause complications.

1. Never expect anything from him, he is
   NEVER-WELL-DO fellow. (incorrect)
   Never expect anything from him, he is
   NEVER-DO-WELL fellow. (correct)

2. He is a **HEART-CHICKENED** fellow.
   He is a **CHICKEN-HEARTED** fellow

3. Mohammed Tughlak was well-known for his
   SILVER QUICK temper.
   Mohammed Tughlak was well-known for his
   QUICK-SILVER temper.

4. He was found **HEART-BROKEN**.
   He was found **BROKEN-HEAR**T.

5. It is totally a **MAKE-BELIEF** narration.
   It is totally a **MAKE-BELIEV**E narration.

6. Although he was rich yet a **SPENT-THRIFT**.
   Although he was rich yet a **SPEND-THRIF**T.

7. I never trust a **NOTHING-GOOD-FOR** fellow.
   I never trust a **GOOD-FOR-NOTHIN**G fellow.

8. The gang of the murderers was **WAIT-IN-LYING**.
   The gang of the murderers was **LYING-IN-WAIT**.

9. In these days of **THROAT-CUT** competition it is not
   easy to promote sales.
   In these days of **CUT-THROA**T competition it is not
   easy to promote sales.

10. In the days of the war he busied himself in
    MONEY-MINTING.
    In the days of the war he busied himself in
    MONEY-MINING.

11. It rained heavily **NEVER** the less he did not stop.
    It rained heavily **NEVERTHELES**S he did not stop.

12. A **DEVIL-DARE** person can go to any extreme.
    A **DARE-DEVI**L person can go to any extreme.

13. Don't be afraid of him, he is a mere
    SCARCE-CROW.
    Don't be afraid of him, he is a mere
    SCARE-CROW.

14. The sage possessed a wonderful **FORESITE**.
    The sage possessed a wonderful **FORESIGHT.**

15. Many **MEN HEARTED-LIONS** died for the freedom of the country.
    Many **LION-HEARTED MEN** died for the freedom of the country.

There are so many exemplifies on the above topic but just name a few.

CHAPTER 14

NARRATION NEGLIGENCES

Many lapses are seen in direct and indirect narration. They can be avoided easily if the rules of narration are followed and no negligence is allowed to creep in.

When the Reporting Verb is in the Past Tense, all present Tenses of the Direct Narration are changed into corresponding Past Tense. When the Reporting Verb is in the Present or Future Tense, the tenses of the Direct Narration do not undergo any change, when the Direct Narration expresses some universal truth, the Tense of the Reported Speech does not change.

The words of Reported Speech expressing nearness in time or place are changed into those of distance. Verbs like "*shall*", "*can*", "*may*", "*do*" etc. are changed into past tense. If there is an object after the Reporting Verb then "*said*" is changed into "*told*". The Pronouns and Possessives are also changed according to the sense of the sentence.

In reporting questions the Indirect Narration is introduced by such Verbs as "*asked*", "*enquired*" in place of "*said*", "*told*". In reporting imperative sentences, the Reporting Narration is introduced by some such verbs as express command or request.

In reporting exclamatory sentences the Indirect Narration is introduced by some such verbs are express wish, desire, etc. In the Direct Narration the inverted commas are removed.

Below are given sentences showing errors generally committed in Narration.

A) Nancy said that she **IS** always with him. (incorrect)
    Nancy said the she **WAS** always with him. (correct)

B) The teacher said that the sun **SET** in the west.
    The teacher said that the sun **SETS** in the west.

C) The preacher said that the honesty **WAS** the best policy.
    The preacher said that the honesty **IS** the best policy.

D) He **SAID TO ME** that he was reading a book.
    He **TOLD ME THAT** he was reading a book.

E) Josephin told **I** that I should work hard.
    Josephin told **ME** that I should work hard.

F) He asked what **IS** my name.
    He asked what **WAS** my name.

G) The watchman **TOLD** where he **IS** going.
    The watchman **ASKED** where he **WAS** going.

H) The oldman asked Kinsley **WEATHER** he could help him.
    The oldman asked Kinsley **WHETHER** he could help him.

I) You will say that you **HAD** finished your work.
    You will say that you **HAVE** finished your work.

J) Goldy said that she **SINGS** nicely.
    Goldy said that she **SANG** nicely.

K) He said that Purna **HAS** paid them a visit.
    He said that Purna **HAD** paid them a visit.

L) My brother **SAID** to me that he **WILL** come tomorrow.
    My brother **TOLD** me that he **WOULD** come tomorrow.

M) The policeman enquired of him what his name and address **IS**.
    The policman enquired of him what his name and address **WAS**.

N) His guru said where there **WAS** will there **WAS** a way.
    His guru said where there **IS** will there **IS** a way.

O) He **SAID** to his maidservant to come **TOMORROW**.
    He **ORDERED** to his maidservant to come **NEXT DAY**.

P) The boy **TOLD** him if **DID HE REALLY** wanted to see his father.
The boy **ASKED** him if **HE REALLY** wanted to see his father.

Q) The mother **SAID** TO her son to walk fast for it likely to rain heavily.
The mother **URGED** her son to walk fast for it was likely to rain heavily.

R) He **CRIED** that he was undone.
He **EXCLAIMED CRYING** that he was undone.

S) I say to him **POLITELY PLEASE WORK HARD**.
I **REQUESTED HIM TO WORK HARD**.

T) The King **TOLD** his attendents not to leave the palace.
The King **COMMANDED** his attendents not to leave the palace.

U) He **SAID TO** me that Helen came **LAST NIGHT**.
He **TOLD ME** that Helen came **THE PREVIOUS NIGHT**.

V) You told me that **YOU SHOULD** leave the room.
You told me that **I SHOULD** leave the room.

W) The bus-conductor **TOLD** that bus **GOES** to Queen Street.
The bus-conductor **SAID** that bus **WENT** to Queen Street.

X) He asked politely if he **WILL GO NOW**.
    He asked politely if he **WOULD GO THEN**.

Y) He **SAID** they enjoyed **OURSELVES**.
    He **PROPOSED** that they enjoyed **THEMSELVES**.

Z) He **EXCLAIMED** that it **IS** a long queue.
    He **EXCLAIMED WITH SURPRISE** that it was a
    long queue.

CHAPTER 15

Verbs That Vex

A Verb is a word that denotes action, event or a state of being. Sometimes verbs cause a lot of vexation.

Below are given:-

1) It **IS** raining since three o'clock. (incorrect)
   It **HA**S **BEE**N raining since three o'clock. (correct)

2) **GO, FETCH** me some sugar.
   FETCH me some sugar.

3) He was **OVERCAME** by his enemy.
   He was **OVERCOM**E by his enemy.

4) The surface is **FEELING** rough.
   The surface is **FEEL**S rough.

5) If I **SHALL GO** to Kolkata I shall bring an umbrella.
   If I **G**o to Kolkata I shall bring an umbrella.

6) Do you know **TO** play cards?
   Do you know **HOW TO PLAY** cards?

7) Which flower **YOU LIKE** the most?
   Which flower **DO YOU LIK**E the most.

8) I ordered **FOR A** cup of tea.
    I ordered A **CUP** of tea.

9) I, who **IS** her father, shall pay her fee.
    I, who **AM** her father, shall pay her fee.

10) He, who **STAND** there is my bother.
    He, who **STAND**S there is my brother.

11) **HAVE YOU** a spare pen?
    DO YOU HAVE a spare pen?

12) Don't a **FOOL** by fighting against him.
    Don't **BE** A **FOO**L by fighting against him.

13) **I HAVE FORGOT** what he said.
    I **HAV**E **FORGOTTE**N what he said.

14) If he **WILL DISOBEY**, he will be dismissed.
    If he **DISOBEY**S, he will be dismissed.

15) I **HANGED** my coat on the hook.
    I **HUN**G my coat on the hook.

16) No sooner **HE LEFT** the class than they made a noise.
    No sooner **DI**D **HE LEAV**E the class than they made a noise.

17) **I AM HAVE** a new bicycle tomorrow.
    I **AM HAVIN**G a new bicycle tomorrow.

18) I **KNOWED** that he was a policeman in plain clothes.
I **KNE**W that he was a policeman in plain clothes.

19) Pt. Nehru **WAS BORNE** with a silver spoon in his mouth.
Pt. Nehru **WA**S **BOR**N with a silver spoon in his mouth.

20) Remember she has **BROKE** her promisese many times.
Remember she has **BROKEN** he promise many times.

CHAPTER 16

PUNCTUATION OR
THE RIGHT USE OF STOPS

How often we faced to solve the PUNCTUATION uses. It is one of the indeed important elements in terms of writing and expression of the dialogues etc. Get a glimpse of uses and way of tackling the **PUNCTUATION**.

Punctuation is the art of using the proper marks, Stops or Points in the correct places in composition.

The names, of the different points, stops, or marks used for this purpose are:-

Comma, indicated by (,)

Scmicolon, indicated by (;)

Colon, indicated by (:)

Full stop or Period, indicated by (.)

Note of Interrogation, indicated by (?)

Note of Exclamation, indicated by (!)

Brackets, indicated by () or [ ]

Dash, indicated by __

Hyphen, indicated by -

Apostrophe, indicated by '

Inverted commas, indicated by " "

Below are given a few general rules regarding the use of various PUNCTUATION Marks. The learner must, however, remember that these rules are by no means hard and fast and that there are expectations to most of them. No two writers punctuate in the same way. Punctuation is frequently a matter of feeling or style. Moreover, fashions change even in punctuation. The latest trend is to use as few punctuation marks as are absolutely necessary.

<u>COMMA</u> (,)
The **COMMA** represents the shortest pause. Its chief uses in a Simple sentence are the following:-
Between Nouns or Pronouns in Apposition; as— Alexander, the son of Philip, king of Macedon.
But note—No comma is used if the appositional words are defining or restrictive.
But note—No comma is used between adjectives if it would not be possible to insert and
Thus : A tall, stout, red-faced person.
But : A poor little black boy. (No comma)

In a **Compound** sentence short Co-ordinate Clauses are generally separated by a Comma:-

I came, I saw, I conquered.
Men may come, and men may go, but I go on for ever.

But when the two sentences are not expressed at full length or are very closely allied, the comma is omitted:-
I made haste and caught him.
I took up a stone and threw it at the mad dog.

In **Complex** sentences the following rules regarding the use of Commas should be noted:-
-   A Noun Clause is not usually separated by a comma from the Principal Clause:-
    Eg (No one knows when he will come.)
-   But Noun Clauses must be separated from each other by Commas when they are Objects or Subjects to the same verb:-
    Eg (who he was, or why he came, or what he intends to do, will all be found out in time.)
-   An Adjective Clause is not separated from the Principal Clause by a Comma unless it (the Adjective Clause) is rather lengthy:-
    Eg (The man we saw yesterday has come again today.)
-   An Adverb Clause is sometimes separated by a Comma from the Principal Clause:-
    Eg (I will gladly do this, if I am allowed.)

The Comma is omitted if the Adverb Clause is either very short or very closely connected with the Principal Clause:-
Eg (Send me word before you start.)

THE SEMICOLON (;)
The **Semicolon** is used when a greater pause is required than is indicated by the Comma.
Its chief uses are as follows:-
-   To separate constituent parts of a Double sentence from one another:-
    Eg (As Caesar loved me, I weep for him; as he was fortunate, I rejoice at it; as he was valiant,

I honour him; but as he was ambitious, I slew him.

- To separate a series of loosely connected clauses:-
Eg (Reading maketh a full man; speaking a ready man; writing an exact man.)

COLON (:)

The **Colon** shows a shorter pause than a full stop, but a longer pause than a semi colon. It is often used with a dash (-) after it; as, (:-).

It is used:

a) To introduce a quotation or speech.
b) Before examples, enumerations and explanations.
c) To separate two contrasted sentences.
d) To Separate two statement sentences, when one is used to explain something in connection with the other.

FULL STOP OR PERIOD (.)

The **Full Stop or Period** indicates the close of a complete sentences. The sentence following must invariable be commenced with a Capital Letter.

The Full Stop is also used after abbreviations (a short form of a word or phrase); as, A.D. (for Anno Domini); B.L. (for Bachelor of Law); the Hon. (for the Honourable), M.P. (for Member of Parliament),R.M.S. (Railway Mail Service), and Feb. (February) etc.

A tendency nowadays is not to use a full stop after Mr and Mrs as these have come to be accepted as the full spelling.

INVERTED COMMAS (" ")
Inverted Commas, single or double, are used for indicating the beginning and end of a quotation, or of the actual words used by a speaker.
Double inverted commas used
"I shall give you some wool to make a new dress," said the white lamb to the little girl.
Single inverted commas (' ') are generally used when a quotation is inserted within a quotation; as,
'Death before dishonour'.
He said to me, "I correctly understood his remark 'what cannot be cured must be endured'."

EXCLAMATION
An Exclamation (!) is used after words which express anger, surprise, joy, sorrow, or any other sudden emotion; as,

Eg—What a piece of works is man!
Hurrah! What a child! Terrible! How wonderful! What a fine day it is.
Note—it is also used in place of a comma after a vocative when it is emphatic; as, Rascal! You are the one who ruined me!

THE APOSTROPHE

The Apostrophe (') is inserted to show that some letter or letters have been omitted.

    a) In a contracted words; as I've = I have. I'm = I am. Don't = Do not.

The Hon'ble = The Honourable. Tho' = Though

    b) As a sign in the PossessiveCase; as, Afizah's book.

    c) To indicate the plural of certain words, figures and signs; as, 5's; t's. Add four 2's and six 4's.

INTERROGATION

The note of Interrogation (?) is used after a Direct question; as,

What are you doing here?

Is it necessary to walk all the way?

But it is not used after an Indirect question; as,

He asked me what I wanted.

The Note of Interrogation should be used after a polite request if the form of the sentence is interrogative.

Will you please lend me your watch?

Would you mind occupying the next seat?

DASHES(--)

The Dashes has four main uses:-

    a) To mark a break or abrupt turn in a sentence:-

Here lies the great—false marble, where?

Nothing but sordid (dishonest) dust lies here.

b) To mark words in apposition or in explanation:-
   Nothing comes amiss to her nimble fingers—
   spoons and forks as well as purses.

c) To resume a scattered subject:-
   Health, friends position, happiness—all are
   gone.

d) To indicate hesitating or faltering speech:-
   i—er—believe—er—that we shall—er—er.

e) To insert a parenthetical phrase or sentence in
   the middle of a main sentence. Here two dashes
   are required.
   At the age of ten—such is the power of genius
   they could write verses.

BRACKETS ( )

Brackets are used, like a couple of dashes in (e), as
just explained, for inserting a parenthetical sentence in
the middle of a main sentence.

Eg- At the age of ten (such is the power of genius) she
could write verses.

In such cases Double Dashes instead of brackets
can also be used to separate the portion structurally
unrelated to the sentence, as,

David—I don't know why—refused to leave.

THE HYPHEN (-)

A **Hyphen** is used for joining the parts of a compound
word; as, 'bathing-place,' 'a man-eating tiger';
sometimes to indicate a span of years 1914-1918.
Therefore, to show the division of a word; as.
Father-in-law; passer-by; (ii) one-sixth.

It is used to form compounds beginning with a few prefixes, like

ex, co, self, vice, noun, as,

ex-master, co-operate; self-control; vice-principal; non-conductor;

it is used to form compound fractions and compound numerals; as,

three-fourths; twenty-third.

Note-A hyphen, like the dash, is formed by a horizontal line, but the line is shorter.

CAPITAL LETTERS

The chief rules for the use of capitals are given below:-

- The first word of every new sentence and of every new line of poetry should begin with a capital.
- The Pronoun I and the Interjection Oh and O are always written with a capital.
- The first letter of a Pronoun Noun or a Proper Adjective is always a capital.
- All Nouns and Pronouns which indicate the Deity are written with a capital letter.
- The capital is used to begin Direct Narration in a sentence.

CHAPTER 17

STRONG AND WEAK VERBS

The mere distinction between Strong and Weak verb is of academic interest but it does not have any utility in the grammar of sentence pattern. It is necessary to know the three Principal Parts of the Verbs. Without this knowledge tenses and their various forms cannot be farmed.

Let's read—How?

The **Principal** (main) **Parts** of a verb, from which all other forms or tense can be formed are:-

The <u>Present</u> Tense, the <u>Past</u> Tense, and the <u>Past Participle</u>; all the other parts, Active and Passive, can be easily formed from these three. To 'conjugate' a verb is to show its chief parts. These are the chief parts of a verb in English.

Verbs are classified as **Strong** and **Weak** according to the manner in which they form the **Past Tense** and the **Past Participle**.

Have a look on tests of a **Weak Verb.**
    i)   All verbs whose Past Tense ends in a –d or –t— which is not in the Present Tense are Weak:-

Live, live-d. Fan, fann-ed. Carry, carri-ed.
Think, though-t, Sell, sol-d. Flee, fle-d.

ii) All Verbs whose Past Tense is formed by
shortening (not changing) the vowel of the
Present Tense are Weak:-
Bleed, bled. Shoot, shot. Lead, led. Light, lit or
lighted.

iii) All Verbs whose Past Tense is the same as the
Present are Weak:-
Cut, cut. Hurt, hurt. Put, put. Rid, rid. Spread,
spread.

Let up see the tests of **Strong Verb.**
a) All Verbs which form the Past Tense by
changing (not merely shortening) the inside
vowel, and do not add a final –d, or –t, are
Strong:-
Fight, fought (but 'buy, bough-t' is Weak,
because after changing the inside vowel it adds
a final –t). Hold, held. Stand, stood. Sit, sat. find,
found. Drive drove.

b) All Verbs which form the past Participle in –en
or –n are either wholly or partly Strong:-
Wholly. –Draw, drew, draw –n. Shake, shook,
shake –n.
Partly.—Saw, saw –ed, saw –n, Cleave, clef –t,
clov –en.

LIST OF STRONG VERBS

The list of **Mixed Verbs** given under Group III exemplifies the tendency of Strong Verbs to become weak:-

Group I.—Final -n or -en retained in Past Participle.

Present Tense	Past Tense	Past Participle
Arise	arose	arisen.
Bear (produce)	bore	born, borne.
Bear (carry)	bore	borne.
Bid	bade, bid	bidden, bid.
Bite	bit	bitten, bit.
Bind	bound	bounden, bound.
Eat	ate	eaten.
Forbear	forbore	forborne.
Forget	forgot	forgotten.
Forsake	forsook	forsaken.
Give	gave	given.
Go	went	gone.
Grow	grew	grown.
Speak	spoke	speaken.
Strive	strove	striven.
Take	took	taken.
Tear	tore	torn.
Write	wrote	written.

Group II. –Final -n or -en lost in Past Participle.

Present Tense	Past Tense	Past Participle
Abide	abode	abode.
Awake	awoke	awoke.
Become	became	become.
Begin	began	begun.
Behold	beheld	behled, beholden.
Cling	clung	clung.
Come	came	come.
Dig	dug	dug.
Fight	fought	fought.
Find	found	found.
Fling	flung	flung.
Sing	sang	sung.
Spring	sprang	sprung.
Swim	swam	swum.
Wring	wrung	wrung.

Group III. –Mixed Verbs.

Such Verbs are partly Strong and Partly Weak:-

Present Tense	Past Tense	Past Participle
Beat	beat	beaten
Cleave (split)	clove, cleft	cloven, Cleft.
Climb	climbed	climbed.
Crow	crew, crowed	crowed.
Do	did (irregular)	done.
Grave	graved	graven, graved.

Hang	hung, hanged	hung, hanged.
Hew	hewed	hewn
Lade	laded	laden
Melt	melted	molten, melted.
Mow	mowed	mowen.
Prove	proved	proved
Rot	rotted	rotten, rotted
Saw	sawed	sawn.
Seethe	seethed	sodden, seethed.
Sew	sewed	sewn.
Shape	shaped	shaped.
Swell	swelled	swollen.
Thrive	throve, thrived	thriven, thrived.
Wash	washed	washed.
Writhe	writhed	writhed.

LIST OF WEAK VERBS

The mode of adding the suffix of the Past Tense is not uniform.

1) If the Verb ends in **e**, then **d** only is added and not **ed**; as,
   Live, lived (not lived). Clothe, clothed (not coltheed).
   To this rule there is no exception.

2) The final consonant is doubled before ed, provided
   (a) that it is single, (b) that it is preceded by a single vowel, (c) that the Verb is

monosyllabic or has the final syllable accented.

Fan, fanned (not faned), ; drop, dropped (not droped). Compel, compelled; control, controlled.

But in Verb like lengthen, where the accent is not on the last syllable, the Past Tense is lenghthened; in a Verb like boil, where the vowel is not single, the Past Tense is boiled; and in a Verb like fold, where the last consonant is not single, the Past Tense is folded.

To this rule there are very few exceptions. One exception occurs in the final *l*. The final *l* is doubled, even when it is not accented; as travelled (not travelled).

Group I. –Shortening of Inside Vowel; Past Tense in –t.

Present Tense	Past Tense	Past Participle
Burn	burnt	burnt, burned.
Creep	crept	crept.
Deal	dealt	dealt.
Dream	dreamt, dreamed	dreamt, dreamed.
Dwell	dwelt	dwelt.
Feel	felt	felt.
Keep	kept	kept.
Kneel	knelt	knelt.
Lean	leant, leaned	leant, leaned.
Mean	meant	meant.
Sleep	slept	slept.

Smell	smelt	smelt
Spell	spelt	spelt.
Spill	spilt	spilt.
Spoil	spoilt, spoiled	spoilt, spoiled.
Sweep	swept	swept.
Weep	wept	wept.

Exceptional Verbs:—Make, made, made. Have, had, had. Hear, heard, heard. Leave, left, left. Cleave, cleft, cleft. Lose, lost, lost. Shoe, shod, shod. Flee, fled, fled. Say, said, said. Lat, laid, laid. Pay, paid, paid.

Group II.—Changing of Inside Vowel.

Present Tense	Past Tense	Past Participle
Beseech	besought	besought.
Bring	brought	brought.
Buy	bought	bought.
Catch	caught	caught.
Seek	sought	sought.
Sell	sold	sold.
Teach	taught	taught.
Tell	told	told.
Think	thought	thought.
Work	worked	wrought, worked.
Dare	durst or dared	dared.
Can	could	(wanting)
Shall	should	(wanting)
Will	would	(wanting)
May	might	(wanting)

Group III. —Verbs ending in -d or -t.

Verbs ending in **d** or **t** in the Present Tense have discarded the suffix of the Past Tense to avoid the repetition of **d** or **t**.

a) Some Verbs in this group have the three forms (Present Tense, Past Tense, Past Participle) all exactly a like:-

Present Tense	Past Tense	Past Particpile
Bet	bet	bet.
Burst	burst	burst.
Cast	cast	cast.
Cost	cost	cost.
Cut	cut	cut.
Hit	hit	hit.
Hurt	hurt	hurt.
Spit	spit or spat	spit.
Quit	quit or quitted	quit or quitted.
Wed	wed or wedded	wed or wedded.
Knit	knit or knitted	knit or knitting.

b) Other Verbs in this group end in d in the Present Tense, But form the Past Tense and Past Participle by changing d into t. (There are at least seven Verbs in English.)

Present Tense	Past Tense	Past Participle
Bend	bent	bent.
Build	built	built.
Gild	gilt, gilded	gilt.
Lend	lent	lent.
Rend	rent	rent.
Spend	sent	sent.
Spend	spent	spent.

c) Other Verbs of this group have the three forms all alike expect that they shorten the vowel in the Past Tense and Past Participle:-

Present Tense	Past Tense	Past Participle
Bleed	bled	bled.
Breed	bred	bred.
Feed	fed	fed.
Lead	led	led.
Light	lit, light	lit, lighted.
Meet	met	met.
Read	read	read.
Shoot	shot	shot.
Speed	sped	sped.

CHAPTER 18

Miscellaneous Mistakes

1) There were many birds on the tree, parrots
   COOING, pigeons **TALKING**, crows **CROCKING**
   and owls **CHATTERING**. (incorrect)
   There were many birds on the tree, parrots
   TALKING, pigeons **COOING**, crows **CAWING** and
   owls **HOOTING**. (correct)

2) Don't **GRUNT** like a puppy.
   Don't **YELP** like a puppy.

3) He cracked such a joke as we all **EXPLODED** into
   laughter.
   He cracked such a joke as we all **BURST** into a
   laughter.

4) In anger he **CLATTERED** his teeth.
   In anger he **GNASHED** his teeth.

5) The bird **FLATTERED** its wings and then flew away.
   The bird **FLUTTERED** its wings and then flew
   away.

6) He was merry and whistling like **KITE**.
   He was merry and whistling like **BIRD**S.

7) He **SNORES** while awake and **GRUMNLES** while asleep.
He **GRAMBLE**S while awake and **SNORE**S while asleep.

8) The jackals **CRIED** ominously.
The jackals **HOWLE**D ominously.

9) A huge elephant first **GRUNTED** and then saluted us by raising its trunk high.
A huge elephant first **TRUMPETE**D and then saluted us by raising its trunk high.

10) When the man in the ring whipped a lion it **BARKED** aloud.
When the man in the ring whipped a lion it **ROARE**D aloud.

11) I could hear the **CLAPPING** of my heart.
I could hear the **PALITATIO**N of my heart.

12) Mice **TINKLED** and ran in all directions.
Mice **SQUEAKE**D and ran in all directions.

13) A **BUNCH** of girls came to visit the garden.
A **BEV**Y of girls came to visit the garden.

14) A **BUNCH** of judges will decide the case.
A **BENC**H of judges will decide the case.

15) A **GROUP** of musicians played fine tunes.
A **BAN**D of musicians played fine tunes.

16) Convey to him my **JUGFUL** of thanks.
Convey to him my **BASKETFU**L of thanks.

17) Make for me a **BUNCH** of flowers.
Make for me a **BOUQUE**T of flowers.

18) Prepare a **CATALOGUE** of contents.
Prepare an **INDE**X of contents.

19) A **GROUP** of rivers drains the land.
A **NE**T of rivers drains the land.

20) After night's rest she looked as fresh as **SNOW**.
After night's rest she looked as fresh as **ROS**E.

21) When I touched, I found him as cold as **WATER.**
When I touched, I found him as cold as **MARBE**L.

22) A **BAND** of players played football in the field.
A **TEA**M of players played football in the field.

23) A **TROOP** of dancers visited the town.
A **TROUP**E of dancers visited the town.

24) This medicine is as bitter as **CUCUMBER**.
This medicine is as bitter as **GA**LL.

25) These days Rajesh is as busy as **BAT**.
These days Rajesh is as busy as a **BEE**.

26) My love for her is as deep as a **PIT**.
My love for her is as deep as a **WEL**L.

27) The Prime Minister offered a **FEW** flowers on the unknown soldier's grave.
28) The Prime Minister offered a **HANDFU**L of flowers on the unknown soldier's grave.

29) By nature he is as free as **WATER**.
By nature he is as free as **WIN**D.

30) I am as firm as a **STONE** in my decision.
I am as firm as a **ROC**K in my decision.

31) Our maidservant is as gentle as a **GOAT**.
Our maidservant is as gentle as a **LAM**B.

32) He lost all his wealth in gambling, and became as poor as a **HOUSE-MOUSE**.
He lost all his wealth in gambling, and became as poor as a **CHURCH-MOUS**E.

33) The noise was as loud as **EXPLOSION**.
The noise was as loud as **THUNDE**R.

34) His hair was as white as **MILK**.
His hair was white as **SNO**W.

35) By nature he is as fickle as a **PEACOCK**.
By nature he is as fickle as a **WEATHER-COC**K.

36) To my request he turned as deaf as a **STONE**.
To my request he turned as deaf as a **POS**T.

37) The Negro's complexion was as dark as
BLACKBOARD.
The Negro's complexion was as dark as **PITCH**.

38) He brought a **BASKET** of apples for me.
He brought a **BO**X of apples for me.

39) A **COLLECTION** of people greeted him.
A **CROW**D of people greeted him.

40) Give the child a **LAPFUL** of sweets.
Give the child a **MOUTHFU**L of sweets.

41) You love her, **DO YOU**?
You love her, **DON'T YOU**?

42) A lone duck with three **CHICKS** were enjoying itself
in the pond.
A lone duck with three **DUCKLIN**G was enjoying
itself in the pond.

43) Don't count your **HENS** before they are hatched.
Don't count your **CHICKEN**S before they are
hatched.

44) You aren't going to Mumbai, **AREN'T YOU**?
You aren't going to Mumbai. **ARE YOU**?

45) He was with you, **WAS HE**?
He was with you, **WASN'T HE**?

46) He didn't live long here, **DIDN'T HE**?
He didn't live long here, **DID HE**?

CHAPTER 19

Letter-Writing Lapses

It is really a fun to receive letters, but to pen a good persuasive and correct letter is not so easy. We commit many mistakes willy-nilly in writing our letters. Inaccuracy and errors in correspondence reflect not only our carelessness but also lack of consideration towards the person addressed. Correctness is one of the person addressed correctness is one of the hallmarks of an effective letter. A letter is your second-self, an alter-ego. A few mistakes in your correspondence may spoil your image you have built so assiduously, and so long. A mistake may cause misinterpretation and misunderstanding.

Some are follows:

1) MAY 24th, 1985. (incorrect)
   24th MAY, 1985. (correct)

2) 24 MAY, 1987.
   MAY 24, 1987.

3) Mr. Alex Atherton ESQ.
   Alex Atherton ESQ.

4) YOUR'S faithfully.
   YOURS faithfully.

5) Very AFFECTIONATE yours.
   Very AFFECTIONATELY yours.

6) Yours LOVING.
   Your LOVINGLY.

7) Yours TRUELY.
   Yours TRULY.

8) YOUR'S respectfully.
   YOURS respectfully.

9) YOUR cordially.
   YOURS cordially.

10) YOUR'S obediently.
    YOURS obediently.

11) Sincerely YOUR.
    Sincerely YOURS.

12) Yours very FONDLLY.
    Yours very FONDLY.

13) Yours FATERNALY.
    Yours FATERNALLY.

14) GREATFULLY yours.
    GRATEFULLY yours.

15) THANK for your letter.
   THANKS for your letter.

16) THANK you.
   THANKING you.

17) May God GIVE YOU STAEDY and continuous rise.
   May God GRANT YOU steady and continuous rise.

18) Keep up the excellent JOB and win laurels.
   Keep up the excellent WORK and win laurels.

19) This promotion is a STEP-STONE to further rise.
   This promotion is a STEPPING-STONE to further rise.

20) I shall be pleased to come and bless the baby at the QUICKEST.
   I shall be pleased to come and bless the baby at the EARLIEST.

21) Warm CONGRATULATION on your brilliant success.
   Warm CONGRATULATIONS on your brilliant.

22) We ARE LOOKING forward to hearing from you.
   We LOOK forward to hearing from you.

23) I REGRET TOO MUCH for not being in a position keep an appointment.
   I VERY MUCH REGRET for not being in a position to keep an appointment.

24) I am sorry for not ANSWERING your letter earlier.
I am sorry for not REPLYING your letter earlier.

25) We OWE you an apology for disturbing your peace.
We OWE you an apology for disturbing your peace.

26) I don't know how to SAY my happiness on this
auspicious occasion.
I don't know how to EXPRESS my happiness on
this auspicious occasion.

CHAPTER 20

Quick Recaps on grammar portion

Problem Areas

            Coordinating conjunctions

Many problems associated with conjunctions are linked to the fact that when we use coordinating conjunctions they must link two items that have the same grammatical status (i.e., both clauses-including a finite verb—or both phrases). When writers fail to remember this the result is poor English:

He told us about the trip and that he had managed to make a number of important new contacts.

If you break the sentence down diagrammatically, it is easy to see what is wrong:

He told us
- —about the trip (PHRASE)
- —that he had managed to make a number of important new contacts (CLAUSE)

PART-II

A GUIDE TO
ENGLISH IDIOMS AND PHRASES

Idiom—an idiom is a particular combination of words, which has a special meaning that is difficult to guess, even if you know the meaning of the individual words in it. In order to find an idiom in the dictionary, you need to choose the first most important word in it (ignoring words like 'off' and 'the'). You will find the idioms in the idioms section, marked **IDIOMS**.

Phrase—a group of words that are used together. A phrase does not contain full verb or to express something in a particular way.

A

The **A** B C of: The rudiments of.
> He deserves credit for teaching us the **A** B C of grammar.

ABIDE

Abide by: To stick to.
> He must **abide** by the rules.

ABEYANCE

Be in **abeyance**: To be held in a state of suspension.
> The question of upgrading the local Junior High School was held in **abeyance**.

ABOUT

To be **about**: Busy.
> What are you **about**, AFIZAH
To come **about**: Happen.
> It all came **about** in your absence.

Bring **about**: To cause.
> He has brought **about** many changes in the administrative machinery.

Out and **about**: In a position to move about.
> He has recovered quickly and is expected to be out and **about** very soon.

ABOVE

Above board: Fair, without trickery.
> This place is a bit expensive but all is fair and **above** board here.

Above ground: Alive.
> You can count upon me so long as I am **above** ground.

Above par: Higher than the official price.
> The shares of big companies are sometimes sold **above** par.

Above all: More than all.
> He was a poet, philosopher and **above** all, a great patriot.

ABREAST

Abreast of: Keeping pace with.
> One should keep **abreast** of the times.

ABROAD

All **Abroad**: Confusion
> That was too exciting an experience and his mind seems to be all **abroad** with it.

ACCESS

Have an **access** to: Means of approach.
> It was apparent that he has the free **access** to public documents.

ACCORD

Of one's own **accord**: Willing to.
> He never wanted to go there of his own **accord**.

With one **accord**: With unanimity.
> They all went to do the work with one **accord**.

In **accordance** with: In conformity with.
> The soldier carried out his work in **accordance** with the wishes of his general.

ACCOUNT

Account for: To give reason for.
> His slackness in studies **accounts** for his failure.

Accounted of: To be esteemed.
> Harris is **accounted** of highly in his circle.

On account of: Because of.
> He could not take part in the games on account of his ill health.

Give a good account of: to be successful.
> He gave a good account of himself in the final examination.

Take no account of: To ignore.
> He takes no account of his secretary's minor mistakes.

Take into account: To give consideration.
> I had never taken into account of what he had said about smith.

On no account: By no means.
    You should on no account give this drug to him.

On this account: For this.
    On this account he came out successful.

Send to one's account: To put one to death.
    The judgment was declared and the culprit was sent
    to his account.

On all accounts: Considering from every point.
    He seems on all accounts to have acted like a
    mad man.

Find one's account in: To benefit by.
    No matter what the situations are, a business man
    always tries to find his account in.

To bring to account: To hold responsible.
    You will be brought to account for all your mischief.

ACQUAINTANCE

Scrape acquaintance with: To make oneself known to.
    He is quick in scraping acquaintance with
    attractive girls.

ACID

Acid test: Reliable lest.
    Adversity is the acid test of friendship.

ACQUIT

To acquit oneself of: to discharge.
He acquitted himself of his duty successfully.

ADD

Add fuel to: To incite.
His efforts to bring the two warring nations together only added fuel to the fire.

Add insult to injury: To injure as well as insult.
By making fun of his tattered garments, you are only adding insult to injury.

In addition to: Over and above.
In addition to his rare mental ability, he had great moral courage.

ADDICT

Addicted to: Accustomed to some bad habit.
Normally college students are not addicted to drinking.

ADVANTAGE

Have an advantage over: to have pre-eminence over.
Since our armies are stationed stop hills, we have an advantage over our enemies.

Take advantage of: to use for one's own benefit.
You should not take advantage of his leniency.

To advantage: Favourably, clearly.
We should see the snows to advantage though the day is not very clear.

<u>Have the advantage of</u>: To be recognized by a person without oneself knowing him.

> You have the advantage of me; I do not remember ever to have had the privilege.

AFRAID

<u>I'm afraid</u>: I admit with sorrow.

> I am afraid you are not doing your best.

AFFRONT

<u>To offer an affront to</u>: To insult one.

> One member of the opposition offered an affront to the speaker.

AFTER

<u>After all</u>: Nevertheless.

> After all, he was a sincere man.

<u>To look after</u>: to take care of.

> He looks after my house in my absence.

<u>Hanker after</u>: In search of.

> He does not hanker after money.

<u>After one's heart</u>: Of one's own fancy.

> This garden has been laid out after my own heart.

AGAIN

<u>Now and again</u>: Occasionally.

> The inspector visits our school now and again.

<u>Be all oneself again</u>: To be what one was like before.

> Raju was all himself again.

As much again: twice as much.

It is not only five rupees that I gave him but as much again.

AGE

To come of age: To attain majority.

He was enthroned when he came of age.

Age of discretion: To attain an age of discrimination.

As she has reached the age of discretion she can take care of herself.

All agog: To get excited.

The children were all agog to see the clown.

AIR

Hang in the air: Uncertain.

The future of the coalition Government in some states still hangs in the air.

To put on airs: To be proud.

Persons who are deficient in something will normally try to put on airs.

Take air: to be disclosed.

The decision of the Government to impose new taxes has taken air.

To beat the air: To attempt anything futile.

He was simply trying to beat the air right from the beginning.

An air of absurdity: To appear unreasonable.
This project of yours has an air of absurdity.

With a triumphant: With the appearance of a victor.
With a triumphant air he stepped out to address the large gathering.

ALIVE

To look more dead that alive: To look lifeless.
What happened to you? You look more dead than alive.

ALL

All in all: Holding immense power.
The principal is all in all as far as the internal matters of a college are concerned.

All but: Almost.
My speech is all but finished. His house is all but ruined.

All ears: Very attentive.
The story was so interesting that the children were all eras to their teacher.

In all: All together.
There were five men in all.

All moonshine: Foolish.
What he said was all moonshine.

All out: To put in one's best.
   John made an all out attempt to stand first in
   his class.

All over: Thoroughly.
   He is all over with the sick man.

All the better: Better still.
   He plays in the garden all the while.

All Fool's Day: First of April.
   We all play tricks on All Fool's Day.

All round: Adept in many things, in every direction.
   Lobsang has been adjudged as well round
   sportsman.

All the same: Nevertheless.
   Although he acted rude, he was not punished all the
   same. It is all the same to me whether he comes or
   not.

All and sundry: All, without any exception.
   This rule applies to all and sundry.

ALLOWANCE

To make allowance for: To consider.
   While selecting a candidates, you must make an
   allowance for his previous experience.

ALONG

Along with: In company with.
   I saw my brother going along with his friend.

ALOOF

To keep aloof: To keep away.
> Keep yourself aloof from politics.

ALTAR

To lead to the altar: To marry.
> The prince led her to the altar.

AMEND

To make amends for: To compensate.
> You should make amends for what you have done.

AMISS

To take amiss: To take offence at.
> When your brother says something in anger, don't take it amiss.

Not amiss: Not inappropriate.
> When he tried to tease him it was not amiss for him to say some harsh words.

AMUCK

To run amuck: To run about furiously.
> He ran amuck and hit many persons.

ANCHOR

At anchor: To remain fastened by the anchor.
> He boarded the ship yesterday which was at anchor.

ANGEL

Visits like angels: To visit rarely.
> His visits to this place are few and far between like those of angels.

Angels of death: Messenger of death.
Landslide was the angel of death for the people of India in 1947 (Got to do).

ANIMAL

Animal spirits: Full of vigour.
The little boy is full of animal spirits.

Animal magnetism: To hypnotise; to enchant.
He is not a doctor but he practices animal magnetism for curing his patients.

ANIMATE

Animated discussion: Lively discussion.
There was an animated discussion about Tibet in the Assembly.

ANON

Ever and anon: Frequently.
I go to his place ever and anon.

ANSWER

Answer for: Be responsible.
The boy will have to answer for his bad conduct.

Answer to: Correspond.
His behaviour answers to the description of the teacher.

Answer: Serve.
This letter answers my purpose.
The building answers the description.

Mohammed Wasim

<u>To answer</u>: Succeed.
   I think your efforts will not answer.

<u>Answer back</u>: To give an unsavoury or tart reply.
   To your elders, you should not answer back.

ANTIDOTE
<u>Act as an antidote</u>: To care; to neutralize.
Co-operation will act as an antidote to many social evils.

ANTIPODE
<u>To be antipodes of</u>: Diametrically opposite.
   The communists are the antipodes of the capitalists.

ANY
<u>Any the wiser</u>: Not at all wiser.
   He returned from America without being any
   the wiser.

<u>Any number</u>: Large number.
   Any number of boys may have slipped away from
   the class.

ANYTHING
<u>Anything but</u>: Not in the least.
   Your behavior is anything but good.

APART
<u>Like two poles apart</u>: Holding exactly opposite views.
   They are like two poles apart.

APE

To play the ape: To imitate.
>   You cannot increase your knowledge by playing the ape.

APEX

(On) the apex: At the summit of.
>   Human beings stand on the apex of creation.

APOSTLE

Apostle of: Advocate of.
>   Gandhiji was the apostle of non-violence.

APPEARANCE

To put in an appearance: To be present; to appear.
>   You may put in an appearance in our social function today.

APPLE

Apple of discord: Cause of quarrelling.
>   The landed property left by Mr David proved to be an apple of discord among his sons.

Dead sea apple: To be of no use.
>   All my efforts became a dead sea apple.

Apple of one's eye: A dearly loved person; a cherished object.
>   The new baby was the apple of her father's eye.

To upset the apple cart: To shatter one's schemes.
>   His poor health upset the apple cart of his ambitions.

APPLY

To apply oneself to: To devote.

> The primary duty of the students is to apply themselves to their studies.

APPOINTMENT

To keep appointment: To appear in time at the fixed place.

> We must try to keep our appointment.

To break an appointment: Not to meet in time at the fixed place.

> It is not nice of him to break our appointment.

APPREHENSION

Beyond apprehension: Beyond one's power of understanding.

> What he says is beyond my apprehension.

APT

Apt to: Liable to; inclined to.

> Promise made in youthful days are apt to be broken.

APPRENTICE

To bind as an apprentice: A beginner.

> She was bound as an apprentice to a hair-dresser.

APRON

Tied to apron strings of: Controlled by a woman.

> Victor was tied to the apron strings of his wife.

ARAB

Street Arab: A homeless child.
India today abounds in street Arab.

ARCH

Arch enemy: Worst enemy.
Anger is the arch enemy of man.

ARCHITECT

To be the architect: Most important; builder.
King Mahendra is the architect of Nepal.

ARGUE

To argue a person into: To persuade.
He failed to argue his brother into politics.

To argue it away: To get rid of.
The problem of over population cannot be argued away.

ARMS

At arms length: To try to avoid.
Please keep that man at arms length; he is a rouge.

Arm in arm: with arms linked.
They walked arm in arm. Nehru ji and Gandhi ji walked arm in arm.

With open arms: To give a hearty welcome.
They received me with open arms.

<u>To take up arms</u>: To appear for war.
>   Some Africans have taken up arms against the U. N. Forces.

<u>To bear arms</u>: To serve as a soldier.
>   What we want is that every India should bear arms.

<u>To lay down arms</u>: To cease to fight.
>   The Chinese have laid down their arms.

<u>Under arms</u>: To get ready for wars.
>   Thousands of men are under arms.

ART

<u>Black art</u>: Magic.
>   Very few people earn their living through black art.

<u>Have art and part</u>: To be an essential part of.
>   He has no art and part in that affair.

AS

<u>As a rule</u>: Generally speaking.
>   I am, as a rule, against borrowing or lending books.

<u>As if</u>: as though.
>   He looks as if he is a rich man.

<u>As for, As to</u>: In respect of.
>   As for myself, I will take nothing.
>   As to this, he knows nothing.

<u>As it were</u>: So to speak.
>   The teacher is, as it were the guide to his pupils.

<u>As usual</u>: As always.
   He came here in the morning, as usual.

<u>As yet</u>: Uptil now.
   He has not come as yet.

<u>As good as</u>: Equally good.
   This house is as good as yours.

<u>As such</u>: In that position.
   He is a teacher and as such he has many
   responsibilities.

<u>As well as</u>: Also.
   Kolkata is the biggest city of India as well as
   the most crowded.

ASHES

<u>To lay in ashes</u>: To be ruined.
   The whole house lay in ashes.

<u>Sackcloth and ashes</u>: To repent.
   The German nation did not wear sackcloth and
   ashes after their defeat.

AT

<u>At a pinch</u>: In distress.
   He was compelled to accept a small salary as a
   pinch.

<u>At the first blush</u>: At the first glance.
   The problem seems at the first blush as difficult as
   the first one.

117

<u>At a loss</u>: Confused; perplexed.
   I am at a loss to understand his idea.

<u>At bay</u>: To hold back.
   He has the courage to hold the wanted visitors
   at bay.

<u>At a stretch</u>: Continuously.
   It is difficult to walk thirty miles at a stretch.

<u>At a discount</u>: Below par, not appreciated.
   The teacher's status is society is no longer at
   a discount.

<u>At best</u>: In the best possible way.
   He is at best a perfect gentlemen.

<u>At a low ebb</u>: On the wane; decline.
   His name and fame now-a-days is at a low ebb.

<u>At close quarters</u>: Near.
   Please put up at close quarters.

<u>At all costs</u>: At any sacrifices.
   He must do that all costs.

<u>At the cost of</u>: At the expense of.
   The king got everything at the expense of
   his people.

<u>At one's best</u>: To show one's best.
   In today's football match, Bharat was at his best.

At all events: In any circumstances; whatever happens.
 I must finish this work at all events.

At daggers drawn: Bitterly hostile.
 After the father's death the sons are at daggers drawn with one another.

At all hazard's: Inspite of all the risks.
 One should do his duty at all hazards.

At large: Fully free; not confined.
 The elephant is roaming at large.

At length: In details.
 We wanted to discuss the subject at length.

At one's disposal: Under one's control.
 The house is at his disposal.

At one's fingers ends: To know thoroughly,
 He has his lessons at his finger's end.

At one's sweet will: As one pleases.
 He went home at his sweet will.

At one's wits end: Puzzled.
 Raju is at his wits end now.

At stake: In danger.
 His life is at stake.

At the eleventh hour: at the very last moment.
 The doctor came to see him at the eleventh hour.

At sixes and sevens: To be in disorder.
   Everything in my room was at sixes and sevens.

At the outset: In the beginning.
   The little boy was careless at the outset.

At sea: To be perplexed.
   He is at sea; he does not know what to say.

To go astray: To go out of the way.
   If good guidance is not given the young boys are
   sometimes likely to go astray.

ATTENDANCE

To dance attendance on: To flatter.
   The workers dance attendance on their employer.

AUTHOR

Author of: To be the creator.
   He is the author of our misfortune.

AVAIL

To avail of: To take advantage of.
   You must avail of this opportunity.

AWAY

To do away with: to give up; abolish.
   He must do away with his habit of speaking ill
   of others.

To make away with: To kill, destroy or decamp.
   The soldier made away with their enemies.

ASKANCE

To look askance: To look at with suspicion.

He looked askance at the Headmaster's wonderful proposal of staring a night school.

AXE

Axe to grind: To serve one's own purpose.

I just went to see him and I had no axe to grind.

B

BACK

Back out: Break promise or agreement.
   He promised to help him in getting that job and I do not think he will back out of it.

Back up: to support.
   He is always ready to back up his parents.

At the back of: Behind.
   There must be someone at the back of this mischief.

Behind one's back: In one's absence.
   He tried to do all sorts of things behind my back.

To have on one's back: To be burdened with.
   He being the eldest son has many responsibility on his back.

To break the back of: To overcome the main difficulties.
   I have almost broken the back of my job.

To turn one's back upon: To turn away.
   He turned his back upon his brother in trouble.

BACKBONE

Backbone: The chief support.
   Wasim is the backbone of the team.

BAD

Bad blood: Enemity.
>There should be no bad blood among us.

To be in bad odour: To become unpopular.
>Because of his bad habits, he is in bad odour with the decent people.

BAG

Bag and Baggage: Belonging.
>He left the place bag and baggage.

Bag of bones: A very lean person.
>He cannot do any physical work for is a mere bag of bones.

To let the cat out of the bag: To disclose a secret.
>The boy let the cat out of the bag before the teacher.

Whole bag of tricks: every device.
>Our players used the whole bag of tricks to win the trophy.

In the bottom of the bag: A last resources.
>I need not worry for I have something very reliable in the bottom of my bag.

BAIT

To bait a trap: To lure someone into the trap.
>Doctors who guarantee cent percent cure of their medicines are only baiting to trap for the ignorant people.

BALANCE

To lose one's balance: To behave awkwardly.
> After the accident he has lost his balance.

BALL

To keep the ball rolling: To keep things moving.
> Yesterday's meting was a success, for everybody kept the ball rolling.

BANDY

To bandy about: To discuss.
> Do not waste your time by banding about this matter with them.

BANG

Going with a bang: Going just right.
> Here everything is going with a bang.

BARE

Bare of: Devoid of.
> This part of our country is bare of any tree.

BARGAIN

To close the bargain: to come to terms.
> The people of this country are not ready to close a bargain with the rebels.

Into the bargain: Over and above, besides.
> With the horse, he got the new saddle into the bargain.

BARKING

Barking up the wrong tree: to follow a wrong line of action.

>He seems to be barking up the wrong tree.

Bark worse than bite: Anger worse than actions.

>His bark is worse than his bite.

BASK

Bask at: To enjoy sunshine or warmth.

>The old man is basking in the sun.

Bask in: Enjoy favour.

>The boy is basking in her favour like a beggar in the sun.

BATHE

Bathe in: Surround.

>The hills were bathed in the moonlight.

BAY

To bay at the moon: to try something impossible.

>You should not waste your time baying at the moon now.

BE-ALL

Be-all and End-all: Sole purpose.

>Acquiring information is not the be-all and end-all of education.

BEAN

Full of beans: Full of vigour.

>He is full of beans at sixty.

BEAR

To bear the burnt of: To endure the main force of.
> The soldiers in particular, had to bear the burnt of the battle.

To bear a hand: Give help.
> Could you bear me a hand in lifting up this load?

To bear down: To crush.
> The members of the ruling party could bear down all oppositions.

Bear with: To tolerate.
> I could not bear with his not temper.

Bear out: Confirm.
> You will be punished if the evidence bears out the charge.

Bear down upon: To attack.
> The soldiers bore down upon the enemy's hide outs.

BEAT

Beat down: To crush.
> He is out of beat down his foes.

Beat off: to repel an attack.
> You must be prepared to beat off your enemy.

Beat about the bush: To come to the point in a round about way.
> A good lawyer does not beat about the bush.

BEARD

<u>To beard a man</u>: To oppose openly.

We bearded the leader in the hall for his objectionable remarks.

BECK

<u>Beck and call</u>: to be under someone's rule.

He has his own work to do; He can't be at your beck and call.

BED

<u>Bed of roses</u>: Smooth; Comfortable situation.

Life is not a bed of roses.

<u>Bed fellows</u>: Close associates.

In the pleasant and painful situation of life we come across many strange bed-fellows.

<u>To take to bed</u>: To suffer illness.

My mother took to bed yesterday.

<u>Brought to bed</u>: Confined in childbirth.

She was brought to be last week.

<u>Between you and me and the bed post</u>: Confidential.

Don't forget that this is just between you and me and the bed post.

BEE

<u>Bee in one's bonnet</u>: To have some strange and whimsical notion.

Every poet has a bee in his bonnet.

BEFORE

Before long: Soon.

Before long I shall be visiting his place.

BEG

To beg the question: To take for granted the truth of the matter in a dispute.

Your statements that two and two make four is just like begging the question.

BEGGAR

To beggar description: Something which cannot be described adequately.

The scenic beauty of Darjeeling beggars all description.

BEGIN

To begin the world: To start in life.

You are too young to begin the world to-day.

Beginning of the end: First distinct indication of the final result.

The U. N.O's failure to decide many international disputes is not the beginning of the end.

BEHIND

Behind the scenes: To be aware of some hidden motives.

It was only yesterday that I discovered what was going on behind the scenes.

Behind time: Not up-to-date; unpunctual.

You are always behind time.

BELL

Bell the cat: to do a daring job.

Everyone in the school wanted half-holiday but no one was ready to bell the cat.

BELOW

Below one's breath: Silently.

The robbers talked below their breath.

BENT

Bent for: Liking.

She has a bent for with hair-dressing.

BENEATH

Beneath notice: Not worthy of notice.

The picture on the wall was beneath notice.

Beneath contempt: Beneath the dignity; not worth of contempt.

He is beneath contempt.

BENEFIT

Benefit of doubt: Favourable judgement when guilt is not proved.

Since no one could prove his guilt, the court gave him the benefit of doubt and set him free.

BEQUEATH

Bequeath to: to leave one's property to another by will.

He bequeathed to his son a huge amount of money.

BEREFT

Bereft (or Bereaved) of: Deprived of.
> He is bereft of his wife and children.

BEST

To put one's best foot forward: To do one's best.
> After Independence, India has put its best foot forward in the field of agriculture.

Best man: Bridegroom's supporter.
> He acted as the best man in my marriage.

For the best: With good intentions.
> I did that all for the best.

To have the best of: to win in a contest.
> James tried very hard to have the best of me.

To make the best of: To make best use of;
to be contented.
> If you can't have the best, make the best of what you have.

BETTER

You had better: You should better.
> You had better stop doing that silly thing.

Better off: Richer.
> He is better off these days.

BETWEEN

Between two fires: A very disagreeable position.
　　I refused to mediate for I know that I would be put in between two fires.

Between the devil and the deep: To be in a dilemma.
　　He is between the devil and the deep at present.

Between whiles: At intervals.
　　You must take some rest between whiles.

Between the cup and the lip: Something worse may turn up at the end.
　　It is certainty that there is many a slip between the cup and the lip.

Between wind and water: Vulnerable or week point.
　　We must try to attack our foes between the wind and water.

BEYOND

Beyond expectation: superior to; exceeding.
　　What he achieved was beyond my expectation.

BID

To bid fair: Promising
　　She bids fair to be a great artist in future.

To bid adieu: Farewell.
　　He bade adieu to his relatives before going abroad.

BILL

Bill of fare: List of articles of food supplied.
When I visited the restaurant I wanted to have glance at the bill of fare.

Clean bill of health: Without any disease.
He maintains a clean bill of health.

BIRD

A bird of passage: One who does not stick to a job for a long time.
This time he proved himself a bird of passage.

A bird's eye view: General view.
We had a bird's eye view of Kolkata from the New Secretariat (Tower).

BIT

Bit by bit: Slowly.
I will finish my work bit by bit.

Not a bit: Not at all.
He cares not a bit for his studies.

To get the bit between one's teeth: To resist control.
The students have taken the bit between teeth.

BALCK

Black sheep: Faulty; of ill repute.
He is the black sheep of our family.

Blackmail: Money extorted from people by treats.
He was trying to blackmail us.

Black and blue: Thoroughly beaten.

    The police inspector beat the culprit black and blue.

BLAZE

Blaze through: Make known publicly.

    Nehru's name was blazed through the land.

BLIND

Blind alley jobs: Jobs which make persons unfit for anything.

    Copying is blind alley occupation.

BLOCK

Block out: To plan a thing roughly.

    He blocked out the whole job in the beginning of the year.

BLOOD

Blue blood: Honourable descent; noble blood.

    Everyone knows that she is a woman of blue blood.

His blood is up: He is angry.

    It will be foolish if you say something when your blood is up and repent afterwards.

Squeeze blood out of stone: to demand pity from the pitiless.

    He is very stingy; you can't squeeze blood out of stone.

In cold blood: Intentionally; deliberately.

    He committed the crime in cold blood.

Blood and iron: Violent use of force.

    Stalin ruled his country through blood and iron.

BLOSSOM

Blossoming out: Improve; flourish.

    The boy is blossoming out.

BLOW

Blow hot and cold: To show interest at one time and not at another.

    You cannot rely on him; he blows hot and cold while making decisions on trivial matters.

To blow one's own trumpet: To praise one's own deeds.

    He is good in blowing his own trumpet.

Blow off steam: To allow extra energy to escape.

    he plays to blow off steam.

BLUE

Once in a blue moon: Rarely.

    He comes to my house once in a blue moon.

To feel blue: To feel dispirited.

    I am feeling blue these days.

BLUNDER

Blunder way chances: Wasted; make no use of opportunities.

    He has blundered away so many chances.

BLUNT

To blunt the edge of: to weaken the force of.
>   Your kind words will surely blunt the edge of
>   his grief.

BOAT

To be (or sail) in the same boat: To have same risk
or fate.
>   We both are sailing in the same boat.

BODY

Body and soul: Entirely
>   He gave himself body and soul to the fulfillment
>   of his aim.

BOIL

To keep the pot boiling: To make enough to get a living.
>   It is difficult to keep the pot boiling for people of
>   small income.

Boil down: To be reduced to.
>   His lengthy talks can be boiled down to this
>   "hopeless".

BOLT

Bolt upright: Straight.
>   He stood bolt upright when he saw something
>   moving in the bush.

Bolt from the blue: Startling surprise.
>   The news of his death came to me like a bolt from
>   the blue.

BONE

Bone of contention: Cause of dispute.
Viet Nam has become a bone of contention between the two big powers.

Bone to pick: To have something to complain about.
He has a bone to pick with you.

Make no bones: Not to hesitate.
He made no bones about changing his profession.

Feel in bones: With certainty.
He felt what he said in his bones.

BOOT

Heart in one's boots: fearful; lacking in courage.
He had his heart in his boots when he saw the policeman.

Boots: Profit; gain.
It boots you nothing to tell this downright lie.

BORDER

Boarder upon: Amounted to.
His foolish talk boarder upon his madness.

To be born with a sliver spoon in one's mouth: Born is an affluent circumstances.
Tagore was born with a silver spoon in his mouth.

BORN

To be born under a lucky star: To be fortunate.
He is born under a lucky star.

BOSOM

Bosom friend: Intimate friend.
   He is my bosom friend.

Take to one's bosom: To make friend.
   He has taken him to his bosom.

BOTTLE

Bottle up: to keep under strict control.
   The teachers should always bottle up the wicked children.

On the bottle: Not fed by mother.
   She was brought up on the bottle right from her birth.

BOTTOM

At the bottom of: To be the sole cause.
   He is at the bottom of this trouble.

Get to the bottom of: To find out the cause.
   I must get to the bottom of this mystery.

At bottom: In reality.
   He is at bottom a scoundrel.

BOUND

By leaps and bounds: Very quickly.
   She made progress by leaps and bounds.

Bound up with: Interested in our fond of.
   The two brothers are bound up with each other.

<u>Out of bounds</u>: Limit.

    The place is out of bounds for civilians.

<u>BOW</u>

<u>To draw the long bow</u>: To exaggerate.

    The politicians usually draw the long bow.

<u>A bowing acquaintance</u>: Slight.

    I have just a bowing acquaintance with him.

<u>To have two strings to one's bow</u>: Other alternative.

    He being a clever man, has two strings to his bow.

<u>BRAIN</u>

<u>Rack one's brain</u>: To try to remember.

    I am not going to rack my brains now.

<u>Pick one's brains</u>: To make use of one's knowledge.

    For your own benefit, you must try to pick his brains.

<u>Cudgel one's brains</u>: To think seriously.

    You must cudgel your brain to get the correct answer.

<u>On the brains</u>: To be pre-occupied.

    He does not want to play; he has something on the brains.

<u>BREAD</u>

<u>Bread</u>: Livelihood.

    We have to work hard for our bread.

<u>To take the bread out of one's mouth</u>: take away one's living.

It is not good to take away one's bread.

<u>Know on which side one's bread is buttered</u>: To know one's interest.

You are expected to know on which side your bread is buttered.

<u>Bread winner</u>: One who earns a living.

He is the bread winner of our family.

BREAK

<u>Break open</u>: Open forcibly.

The boys broke open the door because they had lost their keys.

<u>Break out</u>: Appear suddenly.

Cholers has broken out in the city.

<u>Break loose</u>: Get away.

My dog broke loose at midnight.

<u>Break up</u>: To come to an end.

Our school will break up for the holidays very soon.

<u>Break the ice</u>: To overcome difficulties.

He tried his best to break the ice.

BREAST

<u>To make a clean breast of</u>: To confess fully.

He made me a clean breast of his faults before his parents.

BREATH

<u>With bated breath</u>: In low breath; anxiously.
>   The prisoner answered every question with bated breath.

<u>To take away one's breath</u>: To surprise; to astonish.
>   His wonderful acting almost took away my breath.

BREATHE

<u>To breathe one's last</u>: To die.
>   The beggar fell into a ditch and breathed his last.

BRED

<u>Bred to</u>: Train.
>   The people here are not bared to mountain-climbing.

<u>Bred in</u>: Nurtured; sunk.
>   Though bred in poverty he comes from a pretty well-to-do family.

BRIDGE

<u>To bridge over</u>: To reconcile.
>   He tried to bridge over their differences.

BRING

<u>To bring down the house</u>: Win universal applause.
>   His fine speech brought down the house.

<u>Bring one round</u>: To help to recover.
>   Everyone believes that good nursing will surely bring him round.

Bring home to: Prove to.
   He brought home to him his fault.

To bring about: To effect.
   Idleness brought about his failure.

Bring to book: Punish.
   He will bring you to book for this mischief.

Bring to bay: To corner.
   The tiger was brought to bay.

BROOD
Brood over (or on): Think long and sadly over something.
   You should not board over your misfortune.

BROWN
Brown study: A state of reverse.
   Wake him up from his brown study.

BRUSH
Brush up: To receive.
   I must brush up my history for the test.

BUCKLE
Buckle to: Work diligently.
   You can do well if you buckle to.

BURN
Burning question: A keenly discussed topic.
   Unemployment is the burning question of the present day.

Burn one's finger: To be in trouble.
He is not trustworthy; you will burn your finger if you go too close.

Burn the candle at both ends: to waste in two ways.
Soon after his father's dead, he began to burn the candle at both ends.

Burn one's boots: To make impossible to go back, to stake everything for success.
I have already burnt my boots to get to the desired goal.

BURY

To bury the hatchet: To make peace.
The two friends buried the hatchet and are now in good terms again.

BUTTER

Butter on both sides: favourable conditions.
You cannot always have your bread butter on both sides.

BUY

To buy a pig in a poke: To do something in hurry.
Let me think for a while; I don't want to buy pig in a poke.

BY

By and by: Soon.
You will come to know more about him by and by.

By and large: In every way.
> By and large, he is the best boy in the class.

By dint of: Owing to; by force of.
> He has achieved a remarkable success by dint of his labour.

By far: Indisputably.
> Ann is by far the best athlete of our school.

By fits and starts: Irregularly.
> You should not work by fits and starts if you want to achieve anything worthwhile.

By fair means or foul: Anyhow.
> He will complete that by fair means or foul.

By no manner of means (Not by any manner of means): Under no circumstances whatever.
> He could; by no manner of means, be punished to death.

C

CALL

<u>**Call** the man in</u>: To summon.

<u>They **call** her Rosy</u>: To name.

<u>He **called** the roll</u>: to cry our loud.

<u>**Call** me at 5 o'clock</u>: To waken.

<u>He **called** for an explanation</u>: To demand.

<u>**Call** in question</u>: To doubt.
    You cannot call in question his sincerity.
<u>**Call** on</u>: Visit.
    I called on you once in the morning.
<u>**Call** attention</u>: To remind.
    He called my attention to the matter.

CANDLE

<u>Not worth the **candle**</u>: Not worth having.
    This job is not worth the candle.

<u>Not fit to hold a **candle**</u>: Inferior incomparable.

There is hardly anyone who could hold the candle to shastri for courage.

CAP

<u>A feather in one's **cap**</u>: Some distinctions earned.

He has done very well in the examination; this has added one more feather to his **cap**.

<u>If the **cap** fits</u>: If the remarks apply.

I have heard so many things about him; let us see if the cap fits.

Cap a story: To be able to produce a better ne.

I can cap your short story.

CAPITAL

Capital work: Excellent work.

Capital crime: Serious crime.

Capital points: Important points.

<u>Make **capital** out of</u>: to turn to one's own advantage.

James always tries to make capital out of another's misfortune.

CARD

<u>On the **cards**</u>: Likely to happen.

A change in the foreign policy of America is one the cards.

<u>Show one's **cards**</u>: To disclose one's intention.

He has not shown his cards to me yet.

House of **cards**: Unsubstantial.
    His scheme was like a house of cards.

To have **cards** in one's hands: To be the matter of the situation.
    Since you have the cards in your hands you need not be afraid of the situation.

To play your **cards** well: Use or misuse of one's means.
    He has achieved a great success by playing his cards well.

CARPET

Carpet knight: Luxurious.
    He has become a carpet knight after his father death.

On the **carpet**: Under consideration.
    Disarmament is on the carpet.

CARRY

Carry off: Win.
    Mr Amitabha Bachan carried off many prizes.

Carry out: Execute.
    You must carry out your teacher's order.

Carry one's point: Overcome obstacles.
    He could carry his point at last.

CAST

Cast aside: To reject.
>   Do not caste aside his suggestion for the
>   improvement of this school.

Cast in one's lot with: To share one's lot with.
>   I would like to cast in my lot with you.

Cast an eye upon: To glance at.
>   You always cast your eye upon beggars.

Cast down: Worried.
>   He is really cast down about his deteriorating health.

Cast into the shade: Make less noticeable.
>   He cast his wonderful stories into the shade.

To **cast** in one's teeth: To make an insult remark openly.
>   He cast it in his brother's teeth that he was a liar.

CASTLE

Castle in the air: Imaginary schemes.
>   All his schemes are just castle in the air.

CAT

No room to swing a **cat**: A very small space.
>   He does not have room to swing a cat.

To see which way the **cat** jumps: To watch someone's
behavior.
>   Public opinion last year was not in his favour, this
>   time we will see which way the **cat** jumps.

CATCH

To **catch** one's eye: To fall under one's notice.

To **catch** a tartar: To come across a stronger enemy.
The Americans seen to have **caught** a tartar in Viet Nam.

CHANGE

To **change** colour: To turn pale.
He **changed** hi colour when his father saw him smoking.

To **change** hands: Change in ownership.
This building has not **changed** hands for the last fifty years.

CHARM

Charmed life: Free from dangers.
He is said to have lived a **charmed** life.

CHEW

To **chew** the cud: To ponder over; to think deeply.
Philosophers always **chew** the cud.

CHICKEN

To be no **chicken**: No longer young.
Don't preach. I am no longer a **chicken**.

To count **chicken** before they are hatch: To be over hopeful.
They have bought some lottery tickets and have started counting **chickens** before they are hatched.

Chicken hearted: Timid.
   You cannot expect him to take big risks; he is a **chicken** hearted fellow.

CHIME

Chime with: Agree.
   His opinion **chimes** with mine.

CHIP

Chip of the old block: One possessing the qualities of his father.
   Abraham is the **chip** of the old block.

CHURCH

Poor as a **church** mouse: Very poor.
   He is poor as a **church** mouse.

CLAMOUR

Clamour for: Demand.
   The thirsty crowd are **clamouring** for water.

CLEAN

To show a **clean** pair of heels: To run away.
   He showed a **clean** pair of heels in the last light.

Clean tongue: Free from filthy talk.
   He has a **clean** tongue.

CLIP

Clip one's wings: To make weak.
   The defence minister **clipped** the wings of the President.

CLOSE

Close-fisted: Stingy.
> He is a very **close**-fisted man.

Come to **close** quarters: to come into conflict.
> The Chinese came to **close** quarters with the Americans.

CLOUD

Under a **cloud**: In suspicion of disgrace.
> He is under a **cloud**.

In the **clouds**: Visionary.
> You will often find him in the **clouds**.

COAL

Blow the **coal**: To excite.
> The general tried to blow the **coal** by his fiery speech.

Call (or haul) over the **coals**: To rebuke.
> The teacher has to call (or haul) over the **coals** when the children try to misbehave.

COCK

Cock and bull story: Improbably story.
> What he said is a **cock** and bull story.

COLD

Cold comfort: Irritating.
> It is **cold** comfort to tell a patient that his disease is not curable.

To have **cold** feet: to be frightened.
>   He cannot lead his men to victory; he has **cold** feet in war,

To give one the **cold** shoulder: To avoid.
>   The audience gave the speaker a **cold** shoulder.

COLOUR

Coloured statement: Exaggerated.
>   His statement was highly **coloured**.

To join the **colours**: To join the army.
>   You can join the **colours** if you fail to do well in the examination.

Coloured by prejudice: False.
>   His account of yesterday's theft was **coloured** by prejudice.

True **colours**: Real Self.
>   He has shown his true **colours** to-day.

With flying **colours**: With credit.
>   He is sure to come off with flying **colours** at his next examination.

COME

Come about: To take place.
>   How did this sort of things **come** about?

Come across: Meet.
>   I have not **come** across such an intelligent student in my life.

Come off: To emerge.
   The Indians **came** off victorious in Ladakh.

Come of: Result in.
   Misfortune often **comes** of idleness.

Come around: To recover from illness.
   He is **coming** round after his recent illness.

Come to hand: Reached.
   His letter **came** to hand day before yesterday.

COMMAND
To **command** respect: To win esteem.
   Honesty **commands** respect anywhere.

COMMIT
To **commit** oneself: To bind oneself with word or act.
   I would have given this book to you but I have
   already **committed** to one of my friends.

CONTRARY
Contrary to: Opposite.
   His behavior is **contrary** to my expectation.

On the **contrary**: On the other hand.
   He is not rude, on the **contrary**, he is a perfect
   gentleman.

CONVERSANT
Conversant with: Familiar with.
   Botany is a science which he is not **conversant**
   with.

CORNER

To drive into a **corner**: Awkward position.

    Your question drove him into a tight **corner**.

To put in the **corner**: To force into a difficult situations; to punish.

    The boy was put in the **corner** by the teacher.

COUNT

Count on: Depend; hope.

    I can **count** on your sympathy.

COUNTENANCE

To keep the **countenance**: To remain undisturbed.

    He could not keep his countenance because he was joking.

Out of **countenance**: Puzzled.

    His harsh words put him out of **countenance**.

COURSE

In due **course**: At the proper time.

    You will get your money in due **course**.

As a matter of **course**: Natural or usual way.

    The notice will come to you as a matter of **course**.

CRACK

Crack of doom: End of the world.

    The blind will see at the **crack** of doom.

Cracking up: Decaying or becoming aged.

    The old man is **cracking** up.

In a **crack**: In a moment.
> He will do his job in a **crack**.

CREEP

Creeps into: To appear stealthily.
> Many errors have creep into his book.

Skin **creeps**: To have a feeling of fear.
> My skin **creeps** when I read ghost stories.

CROCODILE

Crocodile tears: Hypocritical tears.
> Do not shed **crocodile** tears.

CROW

To **crow** over: Boast meanly.
> It is not good to **crow** over a defeated enemy.

At cock **crow**: At dawn.
> We must start at cock **crow**.

To have a **crow** to pluck: To settle something.
> He has a **crow** to pluck with me.

CRY

To **cry** over spilt milk: Useless regrets.
> It is no use **crying** over spilt milk.

Crying need: A necessity demanding particular attention.
> Family planning is the **crying** need of India family.

Cry out against: To complain.

The common people are **crying** out against the rising prices.

CUP

In his **cups**: Drunk.

The poor man is in his **cups**.

Cup was full: Of sorrow or joy.

His **cup** was full.

CURRY

To **curry** favour: To seek favour.

Your behavior shows that you are trying to curry favour with him.

CURTAIN

Curtain lecture: Scolding given by a wife to her husband.

You must go home soon or prepare yourself for a good curtain lecture.

CUT

Cut out for: Fit for.

I was never **cut** out for an administrator.

Cut out: To stop.

He **cut** out smoking altogether.

To **cut** short: To shorten.

He has been asked to **cut** short his speech.

Cut (or stung) to the quick: to cause pain.
Your words **cut** him to the quick.

To **cut** the Gordian knot: To remove difficulties.
By killing him he thinks that he has **cut** the Gordian knot.

Cut dead: To refuse to greet; to insult.
He **cut** his brother dead.

Cuts no ice: Effects little.
Mere paper qualification **cuts** no ice.

Cut off with a shilling: Left with very little legacy.
He expected a good deal from his father but he was **cut** off with a shilling.

Cut to the heart: To get hurt.
He was deeply **cut** to the heart.

Cut a sorry figure: Make a bad show.
The teacher **cut** a sorry figure of Helen in class.

D

DANCE

Dance to one's tune: Do his bidding.
I left that job because the boss wanted me to **dance** to his.

DARK

In the **dark**: Ignorance.
I kept him in the **dark**.

Dark horse: A man whose activities are not known.
We were surprised when the **dark** horse won the first prize in swimming.

DASH

To cut a **dash**: To make a show.
When occasion arises, everyone tries to cut a **dash**.

DEAD

Dead tired (or dog tired): Very much tired.
I am **dead** tired.

Dead against: Opposed to.
I am **dead** against the system of co-education.

Dead alive: Half-hearted.
You must not do your work in a **dead** alive manner.

As **dead** as a door nail: Quite **dead**.
>The patient is **dead** as a door nail.

Dead of night: At midnight.
>He woke me up at **dead** of night.

DEAF

To turn a **deaf** ear to: To refuse to listen.
>He turned his **deaf** ears to all his requests.

Deaf as a post: Quite **deaf**.
>He is **deaf** as a post.

DEAL

Deal in: To trade in.
>He **deals** in books.

Deal with: To behave; to treat of.
>I will **deal** with you severely if you break the school rule.

DEFECT

Defect of one's qualities: Virtues carried to extremes.
>He has the **defect** of his qualities.

DESCENT

Descent on: Attack.
>The Chinese made a sudden **descent** on our check-post.

Descend from: To belong to.
>Nehru **descended** from a very noble family.

DEVIL

Devil-may-care: Carefree, heedless.
  Everybody knows that he is a **devil**-may-care fellow.

Devil to pay: Serious trouble ahead.
  No one knew that there was the **devil** to pay.

Play the **devil** with: To bring to destruction.
  He tried to play the **devil** with him.

Devil's books: Playing cards.
  Good people should never touch the **devil's** books.

To give the **devil** his due: To give due credit to any
person.

DIAMOND

A **diamond** of the first water: A man of sterling worth.
  He was a **diamond** of the first water.

Black **diamond**: Coal.
  India abounds in mines of black **diamond**.

Diamond jubilee: The sixtieth anniversary of one's
works or marriage.
  They celebrated their **diamond** jubilee yesterday.

DIE

Die away: To disappear.
  The bad effect of the disease has **died** away.

Die out: Not in practice.

    The system of child marriage is slowly **dying** out in our country.

Die in harness: To **die** while doing duties.

    Nehru **died** in harness.

The **die** is cast: Final step taken.

    Die hard: To take long time in **dying** old habits die hard.

To **die for**: Desire.

    I am **dying** to read that novel.

DIG

Dig at: A cutting remark.

    In course of his speech, he was **digging** at me.

Dig the grave of: To make a mistake which proves fatal to him.

    He is **digging** his own grave.

DILEMMA

On the horn of a **dilemma**: To be in a difficult position.

    His father's decision to discontinue his education put him on the horns of a **dilemma**.

DILLY

Dilly-dally: Vacillate.

    You must decide now; you should not **dilly**-dally about it.

DIP

To **dip** into: To do something at random.
    You cannot remember your lesson by merely **dipping** into it.

To **dip** into one's purse: To take out something.
    I just tried to **dip** into his purse but found nothing.

DIRT

Dirt-cheap: Very cheap.
    Potatoes is **dirt**-cheap in India.

To flying **dirt**: To abuse.
    The two boys quarreled and were flinging **dirt** at each other.

Eat **dirt**: To put up with insult.
    No man possessing a little bit of self-prestige will eat **dirt** like that.

DISCOUNT

At a **discount**: Not in popular demand.
    These kinds of shoes are at a **discount**.

With a **discount**: Not to believe entirely.
    You must accept his story with a **discount**.

DISGUISE

Put on a **disguise**: Anything worn to conceal or deceive.
    He had put on a **disguise** to frighten his friends.

Blessing in **disguise**: Something which looked like a misfortune.

> Chinese aggression in a way, was a blessing in **disguise**.

Do

Do up: Repair.
> My watch wants **doing** up.

Do with: Go along.
> He simply can't **do** with it.

Nothing to **do**: Have no concern with.
> They do not have anything to **do** with him.

Do without: Dispense with.
> We can't **do** without food.

To have **done** with: To have completed.
> I have **done** with this back breaking job.

To **do** a thing under the rose: Secretly.
> Why should you **do** your work under the rose.

Done to death: Killed.
> He was **done** to death.

DOG

Dead **dog**: A useless man.
> He cannot do anything; he is a dead **dog**.

Dog's life: Miserable life.
    The poor people in our country are living a **dog's** life.

Under **dog**: A subordinate.
    He does not wield any power for he is an under **dog**.

To go to the **dogs**: To be ruined.
    Because of some bad elements in society, our country is going to the **dogs**.

To **dog** the footsteps of: To follow.
    He was surprised to notice an unknown man **dogging** his footsteps all the way home.

Dog cheap: Very cheap.
    Everything was **dog** cheap in our country before the second world war.

Send to the **dogs**: To throw away.
    He is not careful with his money; he is sending everything to the **dogs**.

DOLDRUMS
To be in the **doldrums**: To feel depressed.
    Because of his failure in the examination, he is in the **doldrums**.

DOOR
To lie at one's **door**: To ascribe.
    Everyone knows that the fault lies at his **door**.

<u>Out of **doors**</u>: In the open air.
>Children have their classes out of **doors** at Santiniketan.

DOUBLE

Double-faced: Not sincere.
>Beware of double-faced scoundrels.

To **double**-cross: To cheat.
>He tried to **double**-cross me but failed.

DOWN

Down in the mouth: Depressed.
>She is **down** in the mouth because she failed in the final examination.

Ups and **downs**: Pleasure and pain.
>We all have ups and **downs** in our life.

Up and **down**: To and fro.
>He walked up and **down**.

To **down** tools: To stop works.
>During the strike, the workers **downed** their tools.

DRAW

Drawing in: Getting shorter.
>You must do everything in time because the days are **drawing** in.

Drawing out: Getting longer.
>Days are **drawing** out.

Draw to: Attracted.
He was so gentle, I was **drawn** to him in no time.

DRIVE

Drive into: To urge.
He has been trying to **drive** mw into doing it.

To **drive** nail home: To silence a person.
By using a few harsh words to him, I **drove** the nail home.

DROP

Drop in: To visit casually.
I **dropped** at your place yesterday.

Drop out: To cease to take part.
Everybody ran round the filed three times but I **dropped** out after completed the second round.

To **drop** a hint: To give some indication.
I **dropped** a hint about his behaviour but you could not take it.

Drop a brick: To say something tactlessly.
He is a kind of man who always **drops** a brick in course of our discussion.

DRUG

Drug in the market: A commodity which is not in demand.
Flour now-a-days is a **drug** in the market.

DRY

Dry jest: Uninteresting humour.
　　I do not find pleasure in a **dry** jest.

Dry as dust: Not lively.
　　His life is **dry** as dust.

DUCK

To play ducks and darkness: To squander.
　　He has played **ducks** and drakes of his fortune.

Lame duck: One who cannot walk properly, or do well in life.
　　He is a lame **duck**.

Like water off a duck's back: To leave no impression.
　　The effect of Alexander's invasion in India was like water off a **duck's** back.

DUST

To bite the dust: To be defeated in an encounter.
　　We will force our enemy to bite the **dust** if they cause any trouble in future.

To kick up a dust: To create trouble.
　　The Chinese always try to kick up a **dust** on our northern Fortier.

E

EAR

To have an **ear** for: To possess aptitude for something.
He has an **ear** for music.

EARLY

Early bird: Person who gets up early; or one who makes time to do other thing.

As he is an **early** bird, he is sure to shine in life.

EASY

Ill at **ease**: Uncomfortable.

He is always ill at **ease** when he sees his teacher.

Easy virtue: Immoral.

In every society we find women of **easy** virtue.

EAT

Eats beautifully: Of pleasant taste.

This fruit **eats** beautifully.

To **eat** one's words: To retract.

Cowards **eat** their words.

To **eat** humble pie: To apologies humbly.

Though he had said so many things in anger, he was forced to **eat** the humble pie.

To **eat** one's heart: To brood over one's misfortunes.
Many Tibetan refugees are **eating** their hearts out.

To **eat** away: To destroy.
Ambition is like an ulcer that **eats** away the vitals of one's body.

EDGE

To be on **edge**: Excited; nervous.
Students are normally on **edge** in the examination hall.

To set the teeth on **edge**: To irritate.
His behaviour being repulsive, set my teeth on **edge**.

EGG

Egg on: To urge.
Who **egged** you on to do this mischief?

Bad **egg**: Useless person.
He is a bad **egg** of his family.

To put all one's **eggs** into one basket: To risk all in one chance.
I cannot afford to put all the **eggs** into one basket.

EKK

Eke out: To add or supplement.
He **ekes** out his income by doing all sorts of job.

ELBOW

Out at **elbows**: In poor condition.
   After the death of his master, he is literally out at
   elbows.

At one's **elbow**: Near.
   He is your secretary and is therefore expected to be
   always at your **elbows**.

Elbow room: Space just enough for moving.
   We don't have **elbow** room in the office of our
   Headmaster.

ELEMENT

To be in one's **element**: To be in suitable surroundings.
   He was not in his **element** in his new position.

Out of one's **element**: Circumstances not congenial.
   Being married to a very wealthy man, she was quite
   out of **element** in his new house.

ELEPHANT

White **elephant**: Difficult to maintain.
   For him his big building is a white **elephant**.

EMBARK

Embark in (on): Put on board a vessel; to engage in a
new business or affair.
   All of a sudden he **embarked** in a new business.

END

To **end** in smoke: To become fruitless.
   All his efforts **ended** in smoke.

On **end**: A good deal.
   I have not received any letter from him for days on **end**.

To make both **ends** meet: To live within one's income.
   I would better struggle hard to make both **ends** meet than to sink in debt for ever.

At loose **ends**: Not in order.
   You will find everything at loose **end**.

Wrong **end** of the stick: To have wrong idea of something.
   You have got the wrong **end** of the stick.

Odds and **ends**: All sorts of things.
   All odds and **ends** were given to me by him from his box.

ENDOWED

Endowed with: Gifted with.
   She is **endowed** with a beautiful voice.

ENGAGE

Engage manners: Manner drawing admiration.
   Everybody likes him because of his **engaging** manners.

ENTER

Enter into: Engage in.
   He **entered** into a discussion with his friend.

Enter upon: To involve.

> Our country will never **enter** upon a war because it is not in keeping with our national ideology.

EQUAL

Equal to: To be able to cope with.

> He is not **equal** to the job entrusted to him by his brother.

ESCAPE

Escape one's lips: Something which should not have uttered.

> The teacher told his student that he word should not **escape** his lips.

ESTATE

The fourth **estate**: Applied to the press.

> The Prime Minister's statement about taxation has been severely criticized by the fourth **estate**.

EVE

On the **eve** of: The time just before.

> I want to see him on the **eve** of his departure.

EVENT

In the **event** of: If it comes.

> In the **event** of war, it will be our duty to defend our country.

EVER

Ever and **ever**: Always.

> He is gone for **ever** and **ever**.

Ever and anon: Now and then.
 He comes to see me **ever** and anon.

EVERY

Every bit: In every way.
 The wrist-watch was **every** bit as good as this one.

Every now and then: From time to time.
 I have asked my friend to visit my uncle's house **every** now and then.

EXAMPLE

Without **example**: Unparallel.
 The aggression of China is without **example**.

To take **example** by: To copy.
 You should take an **example** by his success.

EXCEPTION

To take **exception** of: At the cost of.
 Do not overwork at the expense of your health.

EYE

Eye-opener: Something that reveals.
 His failure was an **eye** opener to him.

Eye witness: One who sees a thing done.
 I have not done it; he is my **eye** witness.

To keep an **eye** on: To watch carefully.
 He is suspicious character; keep an **eye** on him.

All my **eye**: Not real.
  The story told by him is all my **eye**.

Eye service: Work done only in the presence of the master.
  He renders only **eye**-service to his master.

To cry one's **eyes** red: To weep bitterly.
  When he heard the news of his brother's illness he cried his **eyes** red.

Be all **eyes**: To pay close attention.
  When the English professor enter into the class, the student were all **eyes**.

Set **eyes** on: To see.
  Everybody set his **eyes** on her.

Eye for **eye**: Revenge.
  Germany followed the policy of eye for eye.

Upto the eyes: Deeply absorbed in work.
  For the last few days I am upto the eyes in my work.

To make a person open his eyes: To surprise.
  His dramatic success made me open my eyes.

See eye to eye: To agree completely.
  This is a question on which they do not see eye to eye.

With an eye to: With a view to.

>He struggled hard with an eye to improve his standard of living.

To pipe (put) one's finger in one's eye: To weep.

>You are too old to pipe your finer in your eye like that.

Have an eye for: To have regard.

>He has an eye for music.

Eye-wash: Humbug.

>All his speech is eye-wash.

F

Face

To his face: In his presence.

I will certainly say this to his **face**.

Face to face: In front of.

When produced **face** to **face** with the magistrate, the convict confessed his guilty.

Face: Boldness, courage.

He had not the **face** to ask me for this book because he had already damaged one of my new books before.

Show one's face: To appear.

His house being very near he shows his **face** quite often.

To face the music: To face unpleasant consequences.

If you while away your time now, you will have to **face** the music afterwards.

Save one's face: To evade trouble.

I tried my best to save my face.

To lose face: To lose dignity.

He lost his face in the last election.

To fly in the **face** of: To oppose.
> It will be foolish to fly in the **face** of the government's proposal for taxation.

On the **face** of: In appearance.
> He always displayed courage in the face of danger.

To make **faces**: To make gloomy, sad appearance.
> If you go about making **faces** like this, no one will like you.

FAG

Fag end: The concluding portion; end.
> You will find that story at the **fag** end of this book.

FAIR

Fair and square: Just and right in dealing.
> He is **fair** and square in his dealings.

Fair sex: Women.
> Beauty has not been an unmixed blessing for the fair sex.

A **fair**-weather friend: One who does not help you in difficulties.
> Beware of your **fair** weather friend.

Fair and foul weather: Under all circumstances.
> We must be able to struggle hard under **fair** or foul weather.

To be in a **fair** way: About to accomplish.
> She is in a **fair** way to recovery.

FAITH

Good **faith**: Honest intention.
   I wanted to help him in good **faith**, but he took it otherwise.

FALL

Fall back on: Depend on.
   He has nothing to **fall** back on in his old age.

To **fall** through: To come to nothing.
   All over plans **fell** through because of your carelessness.

To **fall** back: To retreat.
   They **fell** back as the enemy advanced.

To **fall** foul of: To quarrel.
   The two sisters have **fallen** foul of each other.

To **fall** in: To **fall** from above.
   After the heavy shower, the roof **fell** in.

To **fall** in with: To meet.
   During my stay in Mumbai, I **fell** in with two of my relatives.

Fall into: To **fall** into a trap.
   He **fell** into his trap.

To **fall** on: To attack.
   The soldiers **fell** on the enemy at night.

Fall prey to: To be the victim of.
>He is a foul and is sure to **fall** a prey to his designs.

Fall flat: To fail miserably.
>His plains **fell** flat.

Fall to: To begin.
>After play, you must **fall** to your studies.

Fall short: Below one's estimation.
>Her success **fell** short of her brother's expectation.

FANCY

Fancy to: Like.
>I certainly **fancy** the idea of your going abroad.

Fancy price: Extravagant.
>During Christmas you will have to buy everything at **fancy** prices.

FAR

Far cry: A long distance.
>It is a **far** cry to England.

Few and far between: Very rare; not frequent.
>Such cases of child marriage are few and **far** between in India.

Far and near: From all directions.
>People came to attend this meeting from **far** and near.

Far and away: Surely.
   He is **far** and away the best boxer of our school.

Far reaching: Of great magnitude.
   Devaluation has its **far** reaching effects.

FAST

A **fast** man: A wasteful person.
   He is a **fast** elderly person who cares very little
   about his money.

Fast behaviour: Thoughtless; wild.
   He is a man of **fast** behaviour.

FAT

To live on the **fat** of the land: The richest or the best of
everything.
   The capitalists today live on the **fat** of the land.

FATAL

A **fatal** blow: That which causes great harm:
   The death of Nehru was a **fatal** blow to India.

FAWN

Fawn on (upon): To flatter.
   People having a little bit of self-prestige would
   hesitate to **fawn** on anyone.

FEAR

For **fear**: Otherwise.
   Tell the truth for **fear** you should be punished.

<u>**Fear** or favour</u>: Straight forward behaviour.

He does everything without **fear** or favour.

FEAST

<u>**Feast** of reason</u>: Learned discourse.

He being a philosopher always prefers to have a **feast** of reason.

<u>To **feast** of one's eyes on</u>: Delight.

We **feasted** our eyes on his wonderful performance.

FEATHER

<u>To be in fine **feather**</u>: In high spirits.

Our professor is in fine **feather** today.

<u>To **feather** one's nest</u>: To collect riches by dishonest means.

Every person in power tries to **feather** his own nest.

<u>White **feather**</u>: Sign of cowardice.

Gurkhas have never shown white **feather** in the battlefield.

FEED

<u>Off one's **feed**</u>: To have no appetite.

He is off his **feed**.

<u>To **feed** one's eyes on</u>: To satisfy.

One can **feed** one's eyes on the scenic beauty of Darjeeling.

FEEL

To **feel** the pulse: To test.
I asked him about his business just to **feel** his pulse.

To **feel** one's way: To be careful.
After obtaining a new job John has been **feeling** his way carefully.

FENCE

To be on the **fence**: Lacking in firm convictions.
Regarding her stand on Viet Nam, our country is not sitting on the **fence**.

FERRET

Ferret out: To search patiently.
The U.N.O. will surely **ferret** out a solution for a lasting peace in the world.

FIDDLE

Fiddle about: To play with.
Do not fiddle about with that pen.

Fit as a **fiddle**: In the best condition.
At seventy, his father is still as fit as a **fiddle**.

FIGHT

To **fight** shy of: To avoid.
He tried his best to make me his partner in business, but **fought** shy of his brother.

Fight out: To fight till the very end.
The problem of over-population should be **fought** out if self-sufficiency is to be accomplished.

<u>FINGER</u>

<u>To the tips of his **fingers**</u>: Thoroughly; completely.
    Rabindra was an aristocrat to the tips of his **fingers**.

<u>To snap one's **finger** at</u>: To ignore; to despise.
    In democracy the leader can ill-afford to snap their **fingers** at the demands of the people.

<u>**Finger** in the pie</u>: To have a share in.
    Though it is his brother's concern, he definitely has his **finger** in the pie.

<u>My **fingers** itch</u>: To be very impatient.
    As my **fingers** are itching I should not wait for others to come.

<u>FIRE</u>

<u>Full of **fire**</u>: Excited.
    The opposition leader was full of **fire**.

<u>To **fire** out</u>: To scold severely.
    I will **fire** out my servant because he is not sincere.

<u>FIRST</u>

<u>**First** and foremost</u>: Most important.
    The **first** and foremost duty of a student is to respect his teacher.

<u>**First** to last</u>: Till the very end.
    He will stand by me in adversity from **first** to last.

FISH

Make **fish** of one and flesh of another: To make undesirable distinction.

As teachers they should not make **fish** of one and flesh of another.

Fish in troubled waters: To try to gain some advantage during period of unrest.

China always looks forward to **fishing** in the trouble waters.

Other **fish** to fry: To have other things to perform.

You go to picture, I have other **fish** to fry.

A queer **fish**: Eccentric person.

James is a queer **fish** of our class.

Neither **fish** nor flesh: Neither this nor that.

Despite their efforts what they obtained was neither **fish** nor flesh.

There are more **fish** in the sea than ever came out of it: Where there is no scarcity.

FIT

Fit for, to: qualified; suitable.

This milk is not **fit** for drinking.

The pen is fit to be used.

Fit up, out: To equip with necessary articles.

He is busy **fitting** up his house for Christmas.

The new aircraft is **fitted** out for its test flight.

FIX

<u>To be in a **fix**</u>: To be in an awkward positions.
 She is in a **fix**.

FLARE

<u>**Flare** up</u>: To shine out; to suddenly get irritated.
 The fire in the street **flared** up.
 You should not get **flared** up at this trivial remark.

FLASH

<u>**Flash** in the pan</u>: A weak effort.
 He was never serious in his studies and his
 preparation was just like a **flash** in the pan.

<u>In a **flash**</u>: In a moment.
 The whole thing came to us in a **flash**.

FLESH

<u>One's own **flesh** and blood</u>: Relations.
 He is our own **flesh** and blood.

<u>**Flesh** and blood</u>: Human being.
 No **flesh** and blood can tolerate this injustice.

<u>To put on **flesh**</u>: To grow fat.
 He put on lot of **flesh** after his holidays.

FLING

<u>**Fling** out</u>: To rush out.
 He **flung** out of his class room.

<u>To **fling** in one's face</u>: To sneer one with.
 It is not fair to **fling** abuses to his face like that.

FLOG

To **flog** a dead horse: To waste energy on something useless.

> To ask him to do this work is like **flogging** a dead horse.

FLOOR

To have the **floor**: To have the right to speak in debate.

> The communist leader took the **floor**.

FLOWER

Flower of speech: Ornamental language.

> His writing abounds in **flowers** of speech.

FLY

Fly in the ointment: Trivial matter that spoils everything.

> His careless remarks provoked to be a **fly** in the ointment and caused an uproar in the assembly.

To **fly** at: To attack.

> He is innocent and it is no use **flying** at him with such scathing words.

To break a **fly** on the wheel: Unjust; improper; fruitless.

> The policy followed by the Government to put an end to students' indiscipline appears to be like breaking a **fly** on the wheel.

FOLLOW

To **follow** suit: To imitate.

> If a small boy cries in the class, the rest will immediately **follow** suit.

Follow the crowd: To act as most people do.

Good leaders do not always **follow** the crowd.

FOLLY

Height of **folly**: Foolishness.

It was the height of **folly** to let America do what it whishes to do in Viet Nam.

FOOL

Fool's paradise: Happiness based on foolish hopes.

You are living in a **fool's** paradise.

To **fool** away: To idle.

He is just **fooling** away his valuable time.

Fool (of): To make someone a **fool**; to ridicule.

We made a **fool** of him.

Play the **fool**: To jest; to idle.

He is simply playing the **fool**.

FOOT

To put one's **foot** down: To make a firm decision.

He never vacillates and knows when to put his **foot** down.

To put the best **foot** foremost (forward): To make the best of an opportunity.

Whenever the opportunity arises he never fails to put his best **foot** foremost.

FOR

For good: For ever.

He left India **for** good.

FORE

Come to the **fore**: Play a leading part.

If you want popularity, you must come to the **fore**.

Forgone conclusion: Conclusion drawn before hand.

His victory in the next election is a **forgone** conclusion.

FORTUNE

Try one's **fortune**: Take an uncertain **fortune**.

You must make yourself bold and try your **fortune**.

FRAUGHT

Fraught with: Laden with.

The task that you have taken up is **fraught** with grave danger.

FREE

Free and easy: Unrestrained; informal.

Don't be shy, be **free** and easy.

Make **free** with: To take undue liberty.

He always makes **free** with my books.

Free lance: Not attached to any particular party or journal.

Strictly speaking, one cannot be a **free** lance in politics.

FRENCH

French leave: Taking leave without permission or intimation.

> College students often indulge in taking **French** leave.

FRESH

A **fresh** lease of life: Wonderful recovery.

> Everybody thought he would die but God gave him a **fresh** lease of life.

Break **fresh** ground: Exploring something new.

> You will always see him breaking **fresh** grounds in his stories.

FULL

To the **full**: Completely.

> You must do your work thoroughly and to the **full**.

Full to oneself: Vainglorious.

> Some peculiar thing about him is that he is always **full** of himself.

G

GAB

Gift of the **gab**: Fluency of speech.
   Nehru had the gift of the **gab**.

GAIN

To **gain** ground: To progress.
   Family planning is **gaining** much ground in our
   country today.

Gain over: To persuade to one's side.
   A nice gift will surely **gain** him over.

Gain time: To obtain delay by some tactics.
   The warring parties **gained** time during truce.

Gain the upper hand: To come out victorious.
   Violence is **gaining** the upper hand everywhere.

Gain ear: To get favourable hearing.
   Inspite of their best efforts, the labourers failed to
   gain the ear of their manager.

GALL

Gall and wormwood: Extremely annoying.
   John's behaviour to his friends was full of **gall** and
   wormwood.

<u>To dip one's pen in **gall**</u>: To write violently.
　　Writers in modern times are fond of dipping their pen in **gall** in order to create a stir in the minds of the people.

GALLOP

<u>To go at a **gallop**</u>: To go at full speed.
　　Election campaign will go at a **gallop** from next month.

GALLOW

<u>**Gallows** bird (to person)</u>: Fit to be hanged.
　　Everybody knows that he is a **gallows** bird.

<u>To have **gallows** in one's face</u>: Sinister look.
　　The robber has the **gallows** in his face.

GALVANIZE

<u>**Galvanize** into life</u>: To rouse into activity.
　　The speech of Nehru **galvanized** the country's youth into life.

GAME

<u>Make a **game** of</u>: To ridicule.
　　They made **game** of his fashionable shoes.

<u>The **game** is up</u>: The scheme has failed.
　　He said to his partners that the **game** is up.

<u>To have **game** in one's hands</u>: To be sure of success.
　　They never slackened their efforts, though they had the **games** in their hands.

GAMUT

The whole **gamut** of: The entire range.

I studied the whole **gamut** of his lofty ideas and schemes, but found all of them impracticable.

GAP

Stop a **gap**: To make up deficiency.

The second hand car through not good, will surely stop a **gap**.

GASP

At one's last **gasp**: At the point of death.

We have lost all our hopes because he is at the last **gasp**.

GATHER

To **gather** momentum: To **gather** force.

The feeling of insecurity among poor people is **gathering** momentum to-day.

GAUNTLET

To throw down the **gauntlet**: To give challenge.

China has thrown a **gauntlet** to America on the issue of the non-proliferation of nuclear arms.

To run the **gauntlet**: To be exposed to sever criticism.

Menon had to run the **gauntlet** on the issue of Indian reverses in NEFA.

GEAR

In **gears**: In working condition.

My bicycle is still in **gear**.

Out of **gear**: unprepared.

> He couldn't do his best because he was out of **gear**.

GEESE

Geese are swans: To speak proudly of one's own belongings.

> To him all his **geese** are swans.

GENTLE

To **gentle** sex: Ladies.

> He is very popular with the **gentle** sex.

GET

Get wind of: To learn about.

> We could at last **get** wind of the murderer.

Get along: To fare.

> Mr Johnny is **getting** along well with his new job.

Get away: To escape.

> The man **get** away with my pen.

Get over: To recover.

> Among other things, it requires courage to **get** over all our difficulties.

Get through: To pass through.

> You must work hard to **get** through the examination creditably.

Get ride of: To be deprived of; to leave.

> You must **get** ride of that nasty smoking habit.

Get on: To live happily; to put on.
The two brothers cannot **get** on together.
The boy could not **get** his coat on.

Get into: To be placed in a position.
If you behave like that, you will surely **get** into trouble.

Get off: To dismount; to escape.
The prince **got** off the horse.
The boy could not **get** his coat off.

Get the better of: To defeat.
It is difficult to **get** the better of him in argument.

GHOST

Give up the **ghost**: To die.
If he does not stop drinking he will soon give up the **ghost**.

Not the **ghost** of an idea: Anything vague.
I do not have the **ghost** of an idea about his marriage.

GILT

Gilt-edged securities: Good investment.
I wish I could have my savings in **gilt**-edged securities.

Take the **gilt** off the gingerbread: To unmask.
Before being a blind admirer of sadhu for their sacrifices, you must take the **gilt** off the gingerbread.

GIRD

To **gird** up one's lions: To prepare.
> Every citizen should, at this critical juncture, **gird** up his lions to the task of making our country self-sufficient.

GIVE

Give way: To yield; to break.
> The enemies were forced to **give** way.

Give away: To disturbed.
> He thanked her for **giving** away the prizes.

Give out: To announce.
> It was **given** out that the school would reopen in April.

Give over: To abandon, to devote.
> The swiss climbers **gave** over their attempts to get to the top of the Everest.
> The have **given** over to collecting funds for the deprived children.

Given to: Addicted to.
> Many young boys are **given** to drinking or smoking.

Give in: To surrender, concede.
> Press him hard and he will **give** in.

Give rise to: To start, raise.
> The rumour is all stuff and nonsense; I wonder what **gave** rise to it.

To **give** someone a bit:

To **give** a piece of one's mind: To scold, to rebuke.
The teacher **gave** the boy a piece of his mind for being unruly.

Give chase: To pursue.
The police dog **gave** the thief a chase.

To **give** a wide berth: To avoid.
Good students should always **give** a wide berth to rogues.

Give vent to: To allow to escape.
He **gave** vent to his pent up feelings when he met me yesterday.

GLAMOUR
To cast a **glamour** over: To enchant.
She cast a **glamour** over the young boy.

GLANCE
Glance off: To fly off at a slant.
The stone **glances** off my head.

Glance at: A hasty look.
He **glanced** at her ring.

Glance over: To read hastily.
I **glanced** over the letter you gave me yesterday.

GLOVE

<u>To throw down the **glove**</u>: To accept a challenge.
> If you are not a coward, you should throw down the **glove**.

GO

<u>**Go** about:</u> Move about.
> He **goes** about doing nothing.

<u>**Go** by</u>: To proceed.
> This is a nice example to **go** by.

<u>To **go** dry</u>: Non-availability of wine.
> Bombay has **gone** dry.

<u>**Go** through</u>: To read or discuss.
> Let us **go** through the Headmaster's report together.

<u>**Go** between</u>: lies between or a middleman.
> He acted as a **go**-between for the two rival groups.

<u>To **go** mad</u>: To become mad or crazy.
> If you study like this you will soon **go** mad.

<u>**Go** hard with</u>: Press heavily upon.
> It will **go** hard with you if you while away your precious time like this.

<u>To **go** a long way</u>: To be sufficient for.
> This medicine will **go** a long way in keeping your health fit.

To **go** out of one's way: To change the course of conduct.

He had to **go** out of his way to please his clients.

No **go**: No sprits; dash.

There is no **go** in this boy.

Go without saying: Evident fact.

It **goes** without saying that Darjeeling is the most beautiful of all hill-station.

Go back on: To withdraw.

He has no principle to **go** by; he will surely **go** back on his ward.

GOLD

Gold fever: Bent on making money.

In these days of crisis everybody is suffering from **gold** fever.

Gold digger: Money maker.

One wonders how and why ministers have turned out to be **gold**-diggers.

GOOD

Good book: in favour.

He is in the **good** book of his boss.

Make **good**: Compensate.

You should make **good** this heavy loss.

As **good** as: Practically.

He is as **good** as dead.

Goody goody: Outwardly **good**.
>   **Goody goody** people are not always good.

Good offices (to ask for): To solicit favour.
>   It will help you to come out of this predicament if
>   you use the **good** offices of the village head.

With a **good** grace: with pleasure.
>   Tell him to clean the bathroom and he will do it with
>   a **good** grace.

GRAIN

Against one's **grain**: Against one's natural inclination.
>   He is not interested in shooting; it does against his
>   **grain**.

GRAPPLE

Grapple with: Tackle.
>   He is **grappling** with a difficult problem.

GRASP

Grasp at: To seize.
>   Politicians never fail to **grasp** at power.

GRASS

To let the **grass** grow under one's feet: To waste time or
opportunity.
>   Do not let the **grass** grow under your feet if you
>   want to achieve something in life.

Grass widow: A wife whose husband is absent.
>   **Grass** widow is a carefree woman.

Go to **grass**: To retire.
  He has done his job in a magnificent manner; he
  must go to **grass**.

GRAVE

One foot in the **grave**: On the brink of death.
  Everybody wonders why the old man wants to earn
  money with one foot in the **grave**.

Quiet as the **grave**: Silent.
  The whole town was as quiet as the **grave**.

To turn in one's **grave**: To be pained after death.
  Nehru will turn in his **grave** to see India going astray
  from the path of socialism.

GREASE

Grease the palm: Bribe.
  If you want to get your work done easily you must
  grease the palm of the person concerned; so they
  say.

GREEK

To be **Greek**: unintelligible.
  His speech was all **greek** to me.

Greek gift: Something given with intent to harm.
  To students, money will often prove to be a **Greek**
  gift.

GREEN

The **green**-eyed monster: Jealousy.
> Othello became the victim of the **green**-eyed monster.

A **green** old age: Old but full of vigour.
> He still enjoys a **green** old age at sixty.

GRINDSTONE

Hold one's nose to the **grindstone**: Work continuously.
> Being a prison of war he had to hold his nose to the **grindstone**.

GRIST

To bring **grist** to the mill: To be profitable.
> He knew well that his business would bring **grist** to the mill.

GROUND

On slippery **ground**: Difficult position.
> He is standing on slippery **ground**.

Dashed to the **ground**: Ruined.
> All his hopes of promotion dashed to the **ground**.

To hold one's **ground**: To stand firm.
> Our enemies still hold their **ground** despite fierce attack from other side.

Fallen to the **ground**: Unsuccessful.
> All his schemes have fallen to the **ground**.

GROW

Grows on: Becomes influential.
Day by day our country is **growing** on international politics.

Grows up: To become mature.
She is quite **grown** up.

GUARD

On one's **guard**: Alert; vigilant.
Be on **guard** against possible infection.

GUT

Guts (slang): Courage.
This boy has no **guts**.

GUTTER

Gutter-snipes: Neglected children.
India has more **gutter**-snipes today than ever before.

Gutter press: Catering for low tastes.

Gutter press can only earn ephemeral popularity.

H

HABIT

Corpulent **habit**: Bodily constitution; fleshy.
   After operation, Pradhan ceased to be a man of
   corpulent **habit**.

Habit of mind: Mental activity.
   Quick decision is a **habit** of mind worth practicing.

HAIR

To a **hair**: Exactly.
   She resembles my sister to a **hair**.

To split **hairs**: To be over precise in argument.
   It is no use splitting **hairs** on this trivial matter.

Hair-breadth escape: Narrow escape.
   He had a **hair**-breadth escape from being run over
   by a bus.

Not turn a **hair**: Show no sign of nervousness.
   The convict related the true story before the
   magistrate without turning a **hair**.

Keep one's **hair** on: Undisturbed.
   They tried their best to provoke him about he kept
   his **hair**.

Hair stand on end: To be scared or frightened.
    The sight of the mile-post at night made his **hair**
    stand on end.

Against the **hair**: Against the natural inclination.
    To die a coward is against the **hair** of every Indian.

Hair brained: Wild; heedless.
    Unhealthy environment is partly responsible for the
    increasing number of **hair**-brained students today.

HALF

Half seas over: Half drunk.
    You will find him **half** seas over every evening.

Half hearted: With no interest.
    He always does his work **half** heartedly.

Better **half**: Wife.
    He does not care much for his **better**-half.

Do a thing by **halves**: Imperfectly.
    He does not like doing things by **halves**.

Go **halves**: Share equally.
    Let us go **halves**, he said.

Too cleaver by **half**: Far too cleaver.
    Everyone knows she is too cleaver by **half**.

HAMMER

Hammer and tongs: To work vigorously.
>   Albert has worked **hammer** and tongs throughout the term.

Hammer at: To labour continuously.
>   He **hammered** at his mathematics.

Hammer out: Devise.
>   He **hammered** out a plan which everyone accepted.

To come under the **hammer**: For sale by auction.
>   All his properties have come under the **hammer**.

Knight of the **hammer**: Blacksmith.
>   Mechanization of industries has hit the knight of the **hammer** very hard.

To **hammer** and idea into ones head: To make one understand.
>   The teacher tried his best to **hammer** this idea into his head but failed miserably.

HAND

Hand and glove: Intimate.
>   I am **hand** and glove with him.

At **hand**: Near.
>   The I.S.C. Examination is at **hand**.

Give one's **hand** to: To marry.
>   He was pleased to give her his **hand**.

In the **hands** of: Control.
>I have left everything in the **hands** of God.

From **hand** to mouth: Live in poverty.
>He has been living from **hand** to mouth many years.

With a heavy **hand**: Oppressively.
>The government restored peace and order with a
>heavy **hand**.

In **hand**: Under control.
>You cannot take law in your **hands**.

Hand to **hand**: At close quarters.
>The Americans and Viet congs fought hand to **hand**
>in Vietnam.

Pass through many **hands**: To pass on without the
knowledge of the owner.
>The transistor he took from me to repair has passed
>through many **hands**.

Have a **hand** in: A share in action.
>Everyone knows that he had a **hand** in the affair of
>his marriage.

Hand in **hand**: Together
>They always move about **hand** in **hand**.

Lay **hands** on: Seize.
>The poor old woman said that he had no right to lay
>his **hands** on her possessions.

<u>On the one **hand**</u>: Contrasted

<u>On the other **hand**</u>: points of view.
   On the one hand he is very rich and on the other **hand** he is very stingy.

<u>Off **hand**</u>: 1) Without preparation
              2) Unceremonious.

1) Your question is a bit tricky and I cannot answer it off-**hand**.
2) It was not expected of you to say in an off-**hand** manner like this.

<u>Out of **hand**</u>: Out of control.
   The bicycle has gone out of **hand**.

<u>All **hands**</u>: Everybody.
   All **hands** worked hard to build the wall.

<u>Clean **hands**</u>: To be honest.
   He has clean **hands** in this matter and as such deserves no criticism.

<u>A good **hand**</u>: Expert; skilful.
   He is a good **hand** at painting.

<u>To wash one's **hands**</u>: To leave or sever connection.
   Owning to his dishonest dealings, he had to wash his **hands** from service.

Hand and foot: Completely.
> The thief, bound **hand** and foot, was taken to the police station.

To lay **hand** on: To begin.
> Once I lay my **hand** on it, I will finish in on time.

Hand in: To give
> You must **hand** in your application to the manager to-day.

Hand on: To pass over.
> Since the book was not mine, I **handed** it on to its owner.

Hand into: To assist.
> He **handed** his old father into the train.

Hand down: To transmit.
> The father **handed** down his knowledge and experience to his son.

From good **hand**: From a reliable source.
> We heard the terrible news from good **hands**.

HANG

Hang about: Loiter.
> I saw a boy **hanging** about my place yesterday.

Hang on: To persist; to depend.
> He is **hanging** on his sister for financial support.

Hang over: Impending danger.
Trouble **hangs** over us.

Hang fire: To hesitate or delay.
You should not **hang** fire in doing what you have already decided.

Hang in the balance: In suspense, undecided.
Her fate **hangs** in the balance.

Hang heavy: Difficult

Weigh heavy:
In the absence of anyone to talk to, time **hangs** (weighs) heavy on her.

To **hang** by a thread: Sure to collapse.
The patient's life is **hanging** by a thread now.

Hang after: To desire.
He being a business man always **hangs** after money.

HAPPY

Happy-go-lucky: Carefree, easy going.
He is a **happy**-go-lucky fellow.

HARD

Hard cash: Actual cash, coins.
He wants one to pay him in **hard** cash; credit he does not allow.

Hard up: Short for money.
    I am really **hard** up these days.

Hard by: Near
    He works in a factory **hard** by.

Hard words: Unkind words.
    I never expected such **hard** words from him.

Hard time: Tough time.
    The old man is having a **hard** time.

Hard and fast: Rigid.
    There is no **hard** and fast rule as to how a pupil
    should be punished for misbehavior.

Hard of hearing: Almost deaf.
    The old man is **hard** of hearing.

Hard facts: Realities that everyone has to face.
    It cannot be gainsaid that life and death are **hard**
    facts of life.

Hard headed: Practical.
    Nehru was a **hard**-headed politician.

Hard nut to crack: A very difficult problem to solve.
    Unemployment problem is a **hard** nut to crack.

To be **hard** put to: To be in great difficulty.
    Even with his riches he was **hard** put to in life.

HARE

<u>Mad as a march **hare**</u>: To be mad with joy; playful.
When he heard the good news; he was as mad as a march **hare**.

<u>Hold with the **hare** and hunt with the hound</u>: To be on both sides.
A diplomat is one who holds with the **hare** and hunts with the hound.

HARP

<u>To **harp** on the same string</u>: To refer to the same topic.

HARROW

<u>Under the **harrow**</u>: In distress.
He has been under the **harrow** for the past six month.

HASH

<u>To make a **hash** of</u>: To spoil.
He has made a **hash** of his wrist-watch.

HASTE

<u>Make **haste**</u>: Do quick.
Make **haste** or you will miss the train.

HAT

<u>To pass round the **hat**</u>: To called money.
He passed round the **hat** and collected a huge amount.

To raise **hat** to: To salute.
> He being a respectable gentleman never fails to raise his **hat** to his superiors.

HAVE

To **have** it out: To express one's mind clearly.
> This time I am determined to **have** it out with him.

Haves and **have** not's: Rich and poor.
> There has always been a never ending struggle between the **haves** and the have-nots.

Have an eye to: To have in mind.
> **Have** an eye to this dog and make sure that it does not come near you.

To **have** the face to do it: To have the guts to do.
> He **had** the face to do such unpleasant task.

HAY

Make **hay** of: Disorder
> He has made **hay** of my room.

Make **hay**-while the sun shines: To make the most of favourable opportunity.
> He believes in making **hay** while the sun shines.

HAZARD

At all **hazards**: Risks.
> Our people are determined to defend their motherland at all **hazards**.

HEAD

To talk over one's **head**: To talk beyond one's comprehension.

Our professor of psychology usually talks over our **heads**.

Head nor tail: Unable to make out anything.

I could not make neither **head** nor tail of his talk.

Lose one's **head**: To get excited.

He provoked me and I lost my **head**.

Out of one's **head**: From imagination.

I told a ghost story to my class out of my **head**.

A good **head**: Skilled in.

He has a good **head** for mathematics.

Head and shoulder: By force; very much.

He entered the room **head** and shoulder.

John is taller than Harry by a **head** and shoulder.

Over **head** and ears: Completely.

He was over **head** and ears in debt.

Head over heels: Deeply; upside down.

She was **head** over heels in love with me.

He jumped **head** over heels into the water.

To make **headway**: To progress.

He has not made much **headway** this time.

Off one's **head**: To go mad.
>   When he drinks, he often goes off his **head**.

Head off: Prevent.
>   If we remain united we can **head** off any attack from our enemies.

Heads I win and tails you loss: To make impossible demands.

Eat one's **head** off: To worry.
>   Pecuniary problem has been eating his **head** off.

HEAR

Not to **hear** of: To disregard.
>   I am pretty certain that he will not **hear** of such a thing.

Hear out: Hear to the end.
>   You must **hear** him out.

HEART

Heart and soul: Earnestly.
>   You must throw yourself **heart** and soul into the work.

To have the **heart** to oak: To be brave.
>   You need not fear; he has got the **heart** of oak.

Take **heart**: To be encouraged.
>   You must take **heart** in times of danger.

Take to **heart**: TO be pained; mortified.
　　You should never take his remark to **heart**.

Heart to **heart**: Frank.
　　We should have a **heart** to **heart** talk to remove all
　　our misgiving.

To win the **heart** of: To capture.
　　In an incredibly short space of time, David had won
　　the **hearts** of his countrymen.

Lose one's **heart**: To fall in love.
　　You had lost your **heart** to that pretty girl of your
　　class at first sight.

Hearts of **hearts**: Deepest feelings.
　　Though people branded his as a traitor, he was in
　　his **hearts** of **hearts** a real patriot.

Wear one's **heart** upon one's sleeve: To expose one's
inmost feelings openly.
　　When slightly disturbed it is not unnatural for a lady
　　to wear her **heart** upon her sleeve.

Have one's **heart** in one's boots (or mouth): To be
frightened.
　　The moment he saw the fluffy hand advancing, he
　　had his **heart** in his mouth (or in his both).

Hale and **hearty**: Strong.
　　At seventy, he is still hale and **hearty**.

HEATHER

Set the **heather** on fire: To create confusion.
   In town yesterday, the angry mob set the **heather**.

Take to the **heather**: To resist.
   Many religious people take to the **heather** because
   religious laws are sometimes very oppressive.

HEAVE

Heave a sigh of relief: To feel free solace.
   Now the harvesting is over, the farmer will **heave** a
   sigh of relief.

HEAVEN

Heaven and earth: All possible means.
   I shall move **heaven** and earth to get this
   wholesome prize.

Heaven of heavens: An abode of God.
   All good people will go to the **heaven** of heavens
   after their death.

HEEL

On one's **heels**: In close pursuit.
   A strange looking man was on my **heels**.

Take to **heels**: To run away.
   An army never takes to their **heels** from the
   battlefield.

Down (out) at **heels**: In poor circumstances
   Even sixty six years after Independences, the Indian
   peasants are still down at **heels**.

Heel of Achilles: Weak point:
  If you can discover the **heel** of Achilles in your enemies, half the battle is won.

Cool (kick at) the **heels**: To wait for a long time.
  For three hours I had to cool my **heels** at NJP station.

HELL

Hell and heaven: Great.
  There is a difference of **hell** and heaven between these two plants.

Hell for leather: At break neck speed.
  The thief ran **hell** for leather.

HELP

Can't be **helped**: No alternative; nothing can be done.
  You must start right now; it can't be **helped**.

Helping hand: Helper.
  I need a **helping** hand to do this.

HERCULEAN

Herculean task: Task demanding tremendous labour.
  This is a **herculean** task which we cannot possibly undertake to finish.

HERE

Hear you are: An expression used to mean here is the thing you need.
  Here you are, your lost book is found at last!

Here, there and everywhere: In every place.
>You can see human rights being whittled down **here**, there and everywhere today.

Neither **here** nor there: Of no importance.
>You can rest assured that his popularity is neither **here** nor there.

HEW

Hewers of wood and drawers of water: Slaves
>He made his tenants the **hewers** of wood and the drawers of water.

Hew one's way: To make one's way.
>You must **hew** your way for the road to life is strewn with prickly flowers and obstacles.

HEY

Hey day: Youth; period of greatest success.
>It all happened during the **hey** day of my career.

HIDE

Hide one's head: To keep out of sight from shame.
>Because of his own misdeeds, he had to hide his head.

To **hide** one's light under a bushel: To conceal one's talent; try to keep facts secret.
>By not writing anything you are **hiding** your light under a bushel.

HIGH

High and dry: Helpless; uneffected by current affairs.
I simply wonder how they could leave **high** and dry.
You cannot find people living **high** and dry in this
twentieth one century.

High time: Time for doing something before it is too late.
It is **high** time we start our business.

High-minded: Noble.
Thant is a **high**-minded person.

High-handed: Overbearing.
Persons in power usually show their
high-handedness in dealing with their subordinates.

High words: Angry words.
Only **high** words were spoken in the Parliament but
no slippers were thrown.

High and low: Of all ranks; everywhere.
High and low attended the sliver Jubilee of his
wedding.

High living: Rich living.
Some disease is sometimes brought on by **high**
living.

High and mighty: Proud; arrogant
It is money that makes people **high** and mighty.

High life: Mode of life prevailing among upper classes.
High life is not that dazzling as some of us
think it is.

High spirits: Lively.
I found him in **high** spirits.

High-colour: Blush; bright.
When I first met her, she had a bright-colour.

HIMSELF

By **himself**: Alone.
He did it all by **himself**.

HING

Off the **hinges**: In a state of confusion.
They were off the **hinges** in yesterday's party.

HIP

Smite **hip** and thigh: Unsparingly; inflict sever defeat.
Now it is the turn of the opposition to smite **hip** and
thigh.

HISTORY

History repeats itself: Events of similar nature recurring.
If **history** repeats itself; the small shall rise and the
big will surely fall down.

HIT

To **hit** below the belt: To play in a foul manner.
If you want to defeat him in the games, do it by all
means but never **hit** him below the belt.

Hit the nail on the head: To guess correctly or
tell the truth
> When you said she is younger for her age, you **hit**
> the nail on the head.

A big **hit**: Successful.
> The staff concert was a big **hit**.

Hit upon (on): Discover.
> The engineer **hit** upon a new plan.

Hit off: Imitate.
> He is off this part of his teacher to the entire
> satisfaction of his classmates.

HOG

Go to the whole **hog**: To do one's job thoroughly.
> Every citizen is expected to go to the whole **hog** in
> building a new and prosperous India.

HOITY-TOITY

Hoity-toity: Naughty; unruly.
> We have a group of **hoity-toity** people in our
> school.

HOLD

Hold water: Sound.
> His argument do not **hold** water.

Hold a candle to the devil: To help one to do wrong.
> Politicians often accused of **holding** candle to the
> devil.

Hold true: To be valid.
>His mathematical calculation of profit and loss does not **hold** good here.

Hold in readiness: To keep ready.
>American soldiers are **held** in readiness for war in Viet Nam.

Hold one's own: To maintain one's position.
>Indian industrialists are **holding** their own in the teeth of foreign competition.

Hold back: To restrain.
>We must **hold** him back from indulging in such vices.

HOLE

Pick **holes**: To find fault with.
>He always tries to pick **holes** in the lay out of my garden.

Hole and corner: Secret.
>One cannot say off hand whether devaluation is a **hole** and corner business between the parties concerned.

Make **hole** in: Spend a huge amount of.
>He has been making **holes** in my pocket right from the day I met him.

HOMEs

At **home**: To be conversant with; comfortable.

He feels quite at **home** in his new house.

She is quite at **home** in mathematics.

To drive a nail **home**: To convince a person by argument.

He drove the nail **home** by telling him of his moral lapses.

HONEST

Honest penny: To earn by fair means.

You can keep your conscience clear by turning on **honest** penny.

HONOUR

Word of **honour**: Promise.

You will get your book back tomorrow, this is my word of **honour**.

HOOK

By **hook** or by cook: By any means fair or foul.

He will get to the top by **hook** or by cook.

Off the **hooks**: In confusion; disorder.

When the boy heard the sad news he was nearly off the **hooks**.

Drop off the **hooks**: Die.

Sooner or later, everyone will drop off the **hook**.

HOOT

Hisses and **hoots**: A shout of disapproval.

They greeted the communist leader with hisses and **hoots**.

HOPE

Hope against hope: To continue hoping when there is no hope.

He hopes against **hope** that something nice will turn up.

HORN

To take the bull by the **horn**: To face danger courageously.

Indecision at this critical moment will not help you in any way; you must take the bull by the **horns**.

HORNET

Hornet's nest: Source of trouble.

Nagaland has become a **hornet's** nest to the people of India.

HORSE

Ride the high **horse**: Put on airs.

Riding a high **horse** often ends in disgrace.

Look a gift **horse** in the mouth: To find fault with a gift.

Sensible people do not look a gift **horse** in the mouth.

HOT

Hot-headed: Impulsive; rash.

He is a **hot**-headed man.

Get into **hot** water: To be in trouble.
   By helping him I got myself into **hot** water.

HOUR

At the eleventh **hour**: At a late stage.
   The doctor came to see the patient at the eleventh **hour**.

In a good **hour**: In opportune time.
   He left the house in a good **hour**.

HOUSE

House on fire: Rapidly.
   When he is good mood, he works like a **house** on fire.

HUBBUB

Hubbub: Uproar.
   I cannot stand the **hubbub** of traffic.

HUE AND CRY

Hue and **cry**: Clamour; shouting.
   No sooner had they heard the roar of a lion than they raised a **hue** and **cry**.

HUFF

In a belief: To cling to a belief.
   He hugged a belief that his school was the best in this district.

HUMBLE

Humble to the dust: Subdue; bring low.

The Americans have been trying to **humble** the mighty china to the dust.

HUSBAND

Husband one's resources: To use one's means frugally.

A colossal waste can be saved if we **husband** our resources properly.

HUSH

Hush up: To suppress.

The matter was **hushed** up and no one could hear anything about it.

Hush money: Money given silence to somebody.

One can do anything with **hush** money these days.

HUSTLE

Hustle and bustle: Din, noise.

One needs the patience of an ass to put up with the **hustle** and bustle of a city.

I

IDLE

Idle away: To waste time.

You must not **idle** the day away else you will have to repent later.

ILL

Take ill: To feel offended.

This is my brotherly advice and you should not take it **ill**.

It's an **ill** wind that blows nobody good: Misfortune that us harmful to everyone.

All the **ills** that flesh is heir to: Diseases and suffering in life.

Scientists have been endeavouring to find antidotes to all **ills** that flesh is heir to.

IMMEMORIAL

Since time **immemorial**: Beyond reach of memory.

Since time **immemorial** man has been fighting against the forces of nature.

IMPLICATION

By **implication**: Indirectly.

His action, not even by **implication**, are detrimental to national interest.

IN

In as much as: Because.
> **In** as much as he failed to keep his promise, he forfeited his money.

Ins and outs: Complete details.
> He knows all the **ins** and outs of his business.

INCH

By inches: Humble beginning.
> Every gigantic task is done by **inches**.

Every inch: Entirely.
> He is every **inch** a saint.

Within an inch of one's life: Very near to the dead end.
> The convict was thrashed within an **inch** of his life.

INSTANCE

At the instance of: At the request or suggestion of.
> I took up commerce at the **instance** of my father.

INTENTS

To all intents and purposes: Practically.
> To all **intents** and purposes he has become an invalid.

INTEREST

On the interest of: For the good of.
> I had to forego so many things in the **interest** of my family.

<u>Returning a blow with **interest**</u>: With increased strength.
  The Viet Congs are returning the blows with
  interest.

INTERVAL

<u>At certain **intervals**</u>: Not regularly; now and then.
  Last night we could always hear the hooting of an
  owl from our camp at certain **intervals**.

INNUNDATED

<u>To **inundate** with</u>: To flood; overflow.
  I have been **inundated** with congratulatory letters.

IRON

<u>With a rod of **iron**</u>: Rule ruthlessly.
  Aurangzeb ruled the country with a rod of **iron**.

<u>Have too many **irons** in the fire:</u> To have too many
things to do.
  At present he has too many **irons** in the fires and so
  he cannot think of my worries.

<u>In the **irons**</u>: Fettered; chained.
  You cannot put anyone in **irons** on ground of
  suspicion.

<u>A man of **iron**</u>: Firm; strong.
  Patel is known to be the **iron** man of India.

<u>**Irony** of fate</u>: Ill-timed, occurrence of events.
  It was the **irony** of fate that the speed master, bell,
  should be killed in his own car.

<u>ISSUE</u>

<u>At **issue**</u>: In question; dispute.

   We discussed the topic on which we were at **issue**.

<u>Join **issue**</u>: To disagree.

   When the question of country's defence cropped up, the Finance minister joined **issue** with most of his colleagues.

<u>Without **issue**</u>: Without any children.

   He is without any **issue**.

<u>ITCH</u>

<u>**Itching** ears</u>: To be restless to hear.

   Their **itching** ears are simply restless to listen to some pop songs.

J

JABBER

To **jabber** about: To talk too much.
What you people are **jabbering** about?

JACK

Everyman **Jack**: One and all.
"This being an important party everyman **Jack** should be present" he said.

Jack straw: A man without any means.
To all intents and purpose he has become a **Jack** straw.

Jack of all trades: A person capable of doing many things.
In these days to specialization, one can ill-afford to be a **Jack** of all trades and master of none.

JAR

Jar upon one's eras: Irritating harsh noise.
His laugh still **jars** upon my ears.

Jarred against: To collide.
The car **jarred** against the electricity post.

JAUNDICE

To see with a **jaundiced** eye: To be prejudiced; envious.
　　The statement made by him is not fair because he
　　looked at everything with a **jaundiced**.

JAW

Jaw-breaker: A word difficult to pronounce.
　　Chinese names are real **jaw**-breakers.

Hold your **jaw**: Stop talking.
　　Well Jack, hold your **jaw**, or you get out of class.

Fall into the **jaws**: To become victims of.
　　Owing to failure of the rains, the people of Bihar fell
　　into the **jaws** of famine.

JAY

Jay walker: A person who disregards traffic regulations.
　　Jay walkers enable many people die their
　　premature death.

Jaykyll and **Hyde**: Simple person in whom two
personalities alternate.
　　It is rather difficult to understand him because more
　　often than not, he plays **Jaykyll** and **Hyde**.

JEOPARDY

Be in **jeopardy**: To be in danger.
　　The success of the Viet congs put the interests of
　　the Americans in **jeopardy**.

JEST

In **jest**: Not seriously.
   I am not sure whether he uttered those words in **jest**.

A standing **jest**: Object of contempt ridiculous.
   Mao's writings have become a standing **jest**.

JIB

To **jib** at: To refuse to do extra work.
   It is not unnatural for him to **jib** at extra home work.

JOB

Job's comforter: A pretentious comforter who aggravates.
   Adversity is the acid test of distinguishing a real friend from a **job's** comforter.

JOG

To **jog** one's memory: To remind.
   I had completely forgotten about it; it is good of you to **jog** my memory.

JOIN

Join hands with: To be united with.
   When idleness **joins** hands with straight-forwardness, an ulcer in society is created.

Out of **joint**: In confusion.
   Because of internal conflicts everything in India seems to be out of **join**.

JOKE

<u>Practical **joke**</u>: Jokes cracked to ridicule someone.
He loves to play practical **jokes** on his subordinates.

JOLLY

<u>**Jolly** fool</u>: Jovial; happy (used ironically).
He must be a **jolly** fool to do it.

<u>**Jolly**</u>: happiest; memorable.
We had a **jolly** good time yesterday in the park.

JOWL

<u>Cheek by **jowl**</u>: Side by side.
They went cheek by **jowl** to threaten the enemies.

JUGGLE

<u>**Juggle** with</u>: To deceive.
He started **juggling** with words to suppress facts.

<u>**Jump** at</u>: To accept with eagerness.
When somebody showed her lost bag, she **jumped** at it.

<u>**Jumped** up</u>: To shoot up.
The prices have **jumped** up.

<u>**Jumped** to</u>: To come to a quick decision.
He **jumped** to a hasty conclusion.

<u>**Jumped** out of one's skin</u>: To jump out of surprise.
He **jumped** out of his skin when his father saw him smoking.

<u>JUST</u>

<u>**Just** as</u>: Exactly when.

> **Just** as we entered, we saw them coming to great us.

<u>JUSTICE</u>

<u>Do **justice** to</u>: To give one due right or praise to.

> As I was full, I couldn't do **justice** to the dainty dishes.

K

KEEN

Keen as mustard: Enthusiastic.

What we want is a group of young persons **keen** as mustard to do selfless social service.

KEEP

Keep an eye on: To guard.

Keep a watch:

We should **keep** a watch on the movements of some anti-social elements in our country.

Keep open house: Entertain everyone.

He is a man who always **keeps** his house open.

Keep down: To control.

He cannot easily **keep** down his temper.

Keep in the background: To keep oneself in the dark.

I **kept** him in the background so as not be enable him to interfere with my personal matters.

Keep one's balance: To maintain mental stability.

When the students do not get what they want, they cannot **keep** the balance and become unruly.

Keep late hours: Late in retiring to bed.

Good students never **keep** late hours.

Keep off: To prevent; to keep at a distance.
    His umbrella being too old, could not keep the
    rain off.

Keep to: To stick to; adhere to.
    One should always **keep** to one's word.
    Keep to your national dress.

Keep pace with: Keep abreast of.
    He being a race horse, I could not **keep** pace with
    him.

Keep within bounds: To keep oneself within limits.
    It is difficult to **keep** the hungry men within bounds.

Keep track: Follow the course.
    Any educationist worth his salt should **keep** track of
    new trends in the field of education.

Keep the wolf from the door: To avoid death by hunger.
    The teeming millions are fighting to **keep** the wolf
    from the door.

Keep back: Conceal; prevent.
    I cannot **keep** back anything from you.

In **keeping** with: In conformity with.
    Your deeds are not in **keeping** with your words.

KEN

Beyond one's **ken**: Beyond one's power to understand.
    Your political ideas are beyond my **ken**.

KETTLE

Pretty **kettle** of fish: Peculiar state of affair.
  We have pretty **kettle** of fish in Viet Nam.

KEY

Have the **key** of the street: Be shut out for the night.
  If you fail to keep to your word, you will have the
  key of the street for to-night.

Golden (or silver) **key**: Money.
  The golden **key** can open every door.

Key up: Stimulate.
  Reading good books will **key** one up to accomplish
  higher objectives.

KICK

To **kick** at: To resist.
  Students today exhibit the tendency of **kicking** at all
  kinds of restraints.

Kick the bucket: Die.
  The old man has **kicked** the bucket.

Kick up a fuss: To cause a commotion.
  The appearance of an actress on the stage **kicked**
  up a great fuss.

More **kicks** than half pence: More cruelty than
kindness.
  Unlike business, there are more **kicks** than half
  pence in service.

Kick up: To raise.
> The boy when thrashed by his teacher **kicked** up a big row.

KILL

Kill with kindness: Overdoing kind attentions.
> Your kindness will only **kill** your children.

KIN

Kith and Kin: Blood relations.
> He was well looked after by his kith and **kin**.

KIND

In a kind: In a way.
> He nodded in a **kind** which expressed his innocence.

Of a kind: Of special type.
> We had a drink of a **kind**.

In kind: Goods and not money.
> The cultivators had to pay their taxes in **kind**.

KING

King of kings: God.
> You should never bow down to any one except the **king** of kings.

KISS

Kiss and be friends: To reconcile.
> Let us **kiss** and be friends.

Kiss the ground: To humble oneself.
Defeat will surely make his pride **kiss** the ground.

Kiss the dust: Submit humbly to.
Indian forced the aggressors to **Kiss** the dust.

KITE

Fly a **kite**: To gauge public opinion; to raise money.
His sensational article was to fly a **kite** about the prospects of our plans.
Canda is flying a **kite** to help the famine stricken people in India.

KNEE

Fall on one's **knees**: To kneel down.
The lady fell upon her **knees** and begged for his mercy.

Bring a person to his **knees**: Reduce him to submission.
He brought his rival to his **knees**.

KNIFE

War to the **knife**: Mortal combat.
We must wage a war to the **knife** against our enemies.

Knife and fork: To eat well.
He plays a good **knife** and fork.

KNIGHT

Knight of the post: Person giving false evidence.
Money can make many a **knight** of the post.

KNIT

<u>Knit one's brow</u>: To contract the brow into wrinkles when one gets mentally upset.

He **knit** his brow in anger and said something very unpleasant.

KNOCK

<u>Knock about</u>: To wonder about.

He was **knocking** about her just now.

To **knock** one's against: To come into conflict.

It was fortunate that he should **knock** his head against his own well-wishers.

Knock up: To rouse.

Knock me up at 6 o'clock tomorrow.

Knock out: To defeat; to plan.

Jack was **knocked** out in the third round.

I told him to **knock** out a small irrigation scheme for our village.

<u>Knock off</u>: To excel; to surpass.

John will **knock** his nearest rival off in the final examination.

KNOW

<u>Know full well</u>: To know perfectly.

The doctor **knew** full well that the old man would die.

Know how: To understand the ways.

One should go to U.S.A. for the technical **know** how of this trade.

In the **know**: Knowing about.

He is not in the **know** of this accident.

L

LABOUR

Labour: From the pain of child birth.

Sunita was in **labour** sine last night and it was only this morning she gave birth to a bonny son.

Labour under: Suffer.

The poor old man had to **labour** under overwhelming odds throughout his life.

Labour of love: Work done with a sense of love and not with a motive of gains.

You think that I get plenty of money here; no, it has been a **labour** of love to me.

Lost **labour**: Unproductive.

His peace mission was a lost **labour**.

LAID

Laid up with: To be confined to bed with some ailment.

I could not go to school because I was **laid** up with fever.

LAMB

A wolf in **lamb's** skin: A hypocrite.

There are many innocent looking wolves in **lamb's** skin.

LAND

Land at (in): Disembark; to find oneself in a situation.

> We **landed** at Kolkata.

> If you go home now you will **land** in trouble.

Land of living: The earth.

> We must strive to do our best while we are in the **land** of living.

LASH

Lash into fury: To enrage.

> His statement **lashed** everyone in the Parliament into a great fury.

LAST

At long **last**: In the end.

> He did his job well at long **last**.

Last but not least: Mentioned last but not the least in importance.

> I have told you all about my schemes; but **last** but not the least, I will tell you as how we should execute them.

To the very **last**: To the end.

> He maintained his good health to the very **last**.

LATE

Of **late**: Lately.

> He is a good student but has not done so well of **late**.

At the **latest**: Not later than.

    I must see you on Monday next, at the **latest**.

Better **late** than never: To do something even at a last period.

    You should have made your position clear before but it is better **late** than never.

LAUGH

To **laugh** at one's beard: To ridicule.

    He always tries to **laugh** to our beards.

Laugh in one's sleeve: To laugh secretly.

    I **laughed** in my sleeve, when he tried to paint a very rosy picture of his impracticable schemes.

Make oneself the **laughing** stock of: Make oneself an object of ridicule.

    By uttering these vainglorious words he made himself a **laughing** stock.

Laugh away: To dismiss something with laughter.

    He could not but **laugh** away when he made his stupid suggestion.

To **laugh** on the wrong side of the mouth (face): To be made to cry.

    On hearing the unexpected news he **laughed** on the wrong side of his mouth (face).

He **laughs** best who always last: Not to indulge in premature laughter.

LAUREL

<u>To win **laurels**</u>: To win honours.
He has won many **laurels** in the field of sports.

<u>To rest on one's **laurels**</u>: Not to strive any further.
It does not pay you to rest on your **laurels**.

<u>Look to one's **laurels**</u>: Afraid of losing pre-eminence.
Look to your own **laurels** and tell me if you can go so low.

LAW

<u>Be placed above the **laws**</u>: No subjected to any laws.
Dictators are placed sometimes above the **laws**.

<u>Lay down the **law**</u>: To speak or talk dictatorially.
Persons in power often try to lay down the **law**.

<u>Give the **law** to</u>: Force one's will upon.
Parents always try to give the **law** to their children.

<u>To take the **law** into one's own hand</u>: To redress one's wrong by using force.
There was a good deal of confusion when some rowdy elements tried to take **law** into their own hands.

LAY

<u>**Lay** aside</u>: To put away or discontinue; be cheerful.
Lay aside your worries.

Lay bare: To reveal.
   The rains **laid** bare the green fields.

Lay heads together: To confer.
   We must **lay** our heads together and thrash out
   a plan.

Lay by: To preserve for future use.
   One should always **lay** by something for the
   rainy day.

Lay waste: To destroy.
   The enemy **laid** waste the beautiful town.

Lay seize: To beseize.
   The general advanced to **lay** seize to the
   strong-hold of the enemies.

Lay to heart: To give due consideration.
   Lay to heart all that your parent tells you.

Lay great store upon: Value highly.
   They **lay** great store upon his sincerity.

LEAD

Take the **lead**: To act as a leader.
   He was too shy to take the **lead**.

Lead by the nose: Force someone to carry out your
order.
   The have's sometimes **lead** the havenot's by
   the nose.

Lead to: Result in.
    Lying surely **leads** one to trouble.

In **leading** strings: In a state of dependence.
    Most of the undeveloped countries in Asia are the **leading** strings of the west.

LEAF

Turn over a new **leaf**: Change one's conduct for the better.
    After the marriage, he has turned over a new **leaf**.

Take **leaf** out of one's book: To follow the example.
    You must try to take a **leaf** out of your brother's book and work hard.

LEAK

Leak out: To become known.
    The examination question papers **leaked** out.

Spring a **leak**: To let in water through a hole.
    The liner sprang a **leak** all of a sudden.

LEAP

Leap in the dark: To do a hazardous job.
    Without thinking of the consequence he **leapt** in the dark.

LEARN

Learn by rote: To commit to memory without understanding.
    Learning by rote does not help anyone to add something to one's knowledge.

LEAST

<u>In the **least**</u>: In smallest degree.

His advice does not help us in the **least**.

<u>To say the **least**</u>: To put in moderately.

Your attitude towards our family has not been very encouraging to say the **least**.

LEATHER

<u>Nothing like **leather**</u>: One's own goods serves all purposes.

You can try all sorts of things but there is nothing like **leather**.

<u>**Leather** and prunella</u>: Difference in clothes only.

The so-called had and good people these days are **leather** and prunella.

LEACH

<u>Stick like a **leach**</u>: Persistently.

He is sure doing well because he sticks to his job like a **leach**.

LEAVE

<u>**Leave** alone</u>: Allow to remain undisturbed.

Leave me alone, please.

I cannot **leave** my children alone at night.

<u>**Leave** out</u>: Omit.

Leave out this chapter for the examination.

Leave out in the cold: Neglected.

He being a poor servant could not get good medical attention and was **left** out in the cold.

LEFT

Left handed compliment: Double edged.

On my passing the examination he paid me a **left** handed compliment.

LEG

Pull one's **leg**: To befool.

Do not try to pull his **leg** in front of his brother.

Take to one's **legs**: Run away.

The odds were against our soldiers and that is why they had to take to their **legs**.

Stand on one's own **leg**: To be independent.

Everyone of you should try to stand on your won **legs**.

Has no **leg** to stand on: Cannot be supported by facts.

Your theory that tomorrow will take care of itself has no **leg** to stand on.

On one's last **legs**: On the verge of death.

Everyone deserted the old man who was on his last **legs**.

LEGION

Their name is **legion**: A great multitude, numberless.

LEISURE

At **leisure**: At one's ease.

LENGTH

Go to any **length**: To any extent as one desires.
>   I can even go to the **length** of saying that he is
>   a liar.

Length and **breadth** of the land: All over.
>   The news of the passing away of the Prime Minister
>   spread over the **length** and **breadth** of the country.

LET

Let down: To lower.
>   I was about to get the job but my own friend **let**
>   me down.

Let loose: To set at liberty.
>   He **lets** his cattle loose during winter time.

Let alone: To say nothing of.
>   The task is too difficult for a man **let** alone a boy.

Let off: To excuse, to discharge.
>   I am **letting** you off this time but if you repeat it next
>   time you will be punished severely.

LEVEL

On a **level** with: To be on the same footing.
>   As far as money is concerned, he is on a **level** with
>   his brother.

Find one's **level**: Find one's place among equals.
    If you want to fight, you must find your **level**.

LIBERTY

At **liberty**: Free to choose.
    You are at **liberty** to choose anything you like.

LIE

Lie in ambush: To conceal oneself for attack.
    The enemies **lay** in ambush and cut off the supplies.

Lie on one's hands: Finding difficult to pass time.
    Time **lay** on his hands when he was away from
    his home.

A white **lie**: Falsehood prompted by good motives.
    What he said was a white **lie**.

LIEU

In **lieu** of: Instead of.
    The workers were given food in **lieu** of money.

LIGHT

Flood of **light**: Full information.
    The police investigation have thrown a flood of **light**
    upon his activities.

Make **light** of: To treat as a little importance.
    He made **light** of my serious warning.

Bring to **light**: To disclose.
    His research work has brought many new things
    to **light**.

See the **light**: To born or to come.
> He was not at home when his child had seen the **light**.
> The collection of his short stories has not seen the **light**.

LIME

In the **limelight**: Made prominent.
> Zeph, who was an ordinary singer before, is in the **limelight** these days.

LINE

All along the **line**: At very point.
> The truth of his allegation was challenged all along the **line** by every person present in the hall.

Draw the **line**: To refuse to do an act beyond a certain limit.
> You cannot expect me to do everything; I think, I should draw a **line** at this point.

Go over the **line**: To go too far in anything.
> He has got a bad habit of going over the **line** in everything.

LOAF

Loaves and fishes: Personal profits.
> Our leaders simply want to enjoy the **loaves** and fishes of politics.

LOGGERHEADS

Be at **loggerheads**: To quarrel.
> The two brothers are always at **loggerheads**.

LIONS

<u>Gird up the **lions**</u>: To prepare for some importance action.

Let us gird up our **lions** and save our country from destruction.

LONG

<u>The **long** and short of a thing</u>: The gist of the matter.

Well, the **long** and short of the story is that each of us should be prepared for the worst.

LOOK

<u>**Look** down upon</u>: To despise.

Such unsocial behaviour is **looked** down upon by all.

<u>**Look** over</u>: To examine one by one.

I have to **look** over the individual cases personally.

<u>One's **look** out</u>: His duty or business.

It is his **look** out.

<u>**Look** for a needle in a haystack</u>: To look for a small object amidst a crowd of many other things.

There is no use searching your nibs in this room; it is like **looking** for a needle in a haystack.

<u>**Look** out for</u>: To seek.

He has been **looking** out for a job since last month.

LOSE

Losing game: Certain of defeat.
They have been playing a **loosing** game from the beginning.

LOVE

There is no **love** lost between them: They hate each other.

For the **love** of: For the sake of.
Nehru sacrificed everything for the **love** of his countrymen.

LOW

Lowly and the lost: Poor and neglected person.
Gandhiji worked hard for the good of the **lowly** and the lost.

Low brows: Gloomy; not highly intellectual.
He always want to write for the **low** brows.

LURCH

To leave in the **Lurch**: To leave in difficulties.
I cannot expect you to leave your friends in the **lurch**.

LUSTRE

Shed a **luster** upon: To illuminate.
Nehru, Gandhi and Patel are the personalities who shed **luster** upon the history of the Indian struggle for freedom.

LUXURY

In the lap of **luxury**: Luxurious.

Our country passing through a very critical time and we cannot afford to live in the lap of **luxury**.

M

MAD

Mad for (or about): Keenly desirous.

He is **mad** for (or about) a new scooter.

MAID

Maid of all work: Maid-servant.

You need a nice **maid** of all work.

MAIDEN

Maiden speech: First speech.

The **maiden** speech which she delivered yesterday had a far reaching effect on the audience.

MAIN

Main chance: Personal interests.

He being a practical man has an eye to the **main** chance.

Might and **main**: With utmost strength or ability.

The soldiers tried to defend the fortress with might and **main**.

MAKE

Make a fortune: To be wealthy.

He **made** his fortune in a very short space of time.

Make a fuss about: To give undue importance to.

Do not **make** a fuss about this trivial matter.

Make a mess of it: To create confusion; disorder.
   If you do not do your experiments seriously, you will **make** a mess of it.

Make believe: Unreal; artificial.
   The children always live in their own **make** believe world.

Make bricks without straw: To try to make or do something without the necessary material.
   People often try to **make** bricks without straw and repent afterwards.

Make good: To fulfill.
   He will do his utmost to **make** good his promise.

Make up for: To compensate.
   He must study hard in the second term to **make** up for the loss of time in the beginning of the year.

MAN

Man in the street: Normal; average man.
   Modern writers do not write for the **man** in the street.

Man of straw: An unreliable person; worthless.
   No one attaches any importance to what he says because everybody thinks that he is a **man** of straw.

Man of parts: Talented person.
   He being a **man** of parts could find no difficulty in solving this intricate problem.

MANNER

After one's **manner**: As usual.
>   The Principal, after his **manner** spoke harshly to one of his servants.

In a **manner**: To some extent.
>   He is, in a **manner**, an independent man.

MANY

Many a time: Many times.
>   **Many** a time have I seen this charming woman.

MAP

Off the **map**: Lose one's prominence.
>   As far as the literary activity is concerned, he is off the **map**.

On the **map**: To be in an important position.
>   Victory in the Second World War has put Germany on the **map**.

MAR

Make or **mar**: Make or destroy.
>   Poverty either makes or **mars** one's career.

MARE

Mare's nest: Absurd discovery.
>   To his great surprise he found out that what he actually discovered was a **mare's** nest.

MARK

Beside the **mark**: Irrelevant; not appropriate.
>   What he said was beside the **mark**.

Make or leave one's **mark**: To leave a lasting impression.

Wherever he went he has left (or made) his **mark**.

Wide of the **mark**: Far from the object aimed at; not to the point.

The statement he made before the lawyer was wide of the **mark**.

MARKET

To bring one's eggs (or hogs) to a bad **market**: To fail one's schemes.

It remains to be seen whether the communist in India would bring their hogs in a bad **market**.

MARROW

The very **marrow** of: The essence of.

You must read the Vedas if you want to get some glimpses into the very **marrow** of the Indian religions and social life.

MASS

In the **mass**: On the whole.

In the **mass**, human life is a never-ending tale of victories and defeats.

MASTER

Be **master** of: Have control over.

He made himself the **master** of his own destiny.

MATTER

<u>For that **matter**</u>: As far as that is concerned.
> He has been very cruel to me and for that **matter** I have lost all hopes of getting anything from him.

<u>In the **matter** of</u>: In regard to.
> He tried his level best in the **matter** of improving the finance of the institution.

<u>**Matter** of fact</u>: Real, practical.
> He being a **matter** of fact person, all his ideas appeared to be logically sound.

<u>To mince a **matter**</u>: To suppress or exaggerate things.
> For fear of punishment he was forced to mince the **matter**.

MEANS

<u>By no **means**</u>: Not at all.
> He is by no **means**, a student of mediocre ability.

<u>By all **means**</u>: Certainly.
> You can use pen by all **means**.

MEASURE

<u>**Measure** one's length</u>: Fall on the ground.
> While trying to escape from the window, the thief **measured** his length on the ground.

<u>Take the **measure**</u>: To ascertain.
> Before taking this drastic action the dictator had taken the **measure** of the situation.

Beyond **measure**: Excessively.
   The loss he suffered was beyond **measure**.

MEET

Meet with: Encounter, come across.
   He knew, he would **meet** with much opposition.

Meet the ear (or eye): To attract.
   The sweet song of the birds **met** the ears of
   travellers.

Meet half-way: To make mutual concessions.
   I am ready to **meet** him half-way if he is willing to
   change his viewpoint.

MEMORY

Within the living **memory**: People living can still
recollect.
   Worshipping of teachers by students is still within
   the living **memory**.

METTLE

On one's **mettle**: To stimulate a person to do his best.
   A wholesome prize put him on his **mettle**.

MILK

Milk of human kindness: Natural kindness, compassion.
   His mother's heart overflows with the **milk** of human
   kindness.

Milk and honey: Abundant means of enjoyment.
   Once our country overflowed with **milk** and honey.

MILL

<u>Go through the **mill**</u>: To undergo unpleasant experiences.

> In order to accomplish his objective he had to go through the **mill**.

<u>**Mill**-stone round one's neck</u>: A great burden.

> He has become a **mill**-stone round his father's neck.

MIND

<u>Bear in **mind**</u>: To remember.

> Bear in your **mind** that dishonesty does pay.

<u>Be in two **minds**</u>: To be undecided.

> You won't be able to achieve success if you are in two **minds**.

<u>Have a **mind**</u>: To be inclined to continue.

> I have a **mind** to continue my studies after my graduation.

<u>To speak one's **mind**</u>: To speak openly.

> Please don't hesitate to speak your **mind** if there is anything you are not satisfied with.

<u>To make up one's **mind**</u>: To decide a course of action.

> He had made up his **mind** to go to his friend's house.

Open one's **mind**: To unburden one's feelings.
When subjected to harsh treatment from her husband the woman opened her **mind** to her brother.

MOMENT

On the spur of the **moment**: Done without previous thought.
He said that they could not expect him to coin a word on the spur of the **moment**.

One's last **moment**: At the time of death.
The old man in his last **moment** asked for a picture of JESUS.

Of great **moment**: Of great importance.
War in Viet Nam is a matter of great **moment** today.

MONEY

Money's worth: Worth the money paid.
The shop-keeper told his customer when the latter complained about the quantity of goods sold, "Don't worry, Sir, you will get your **money's** worth".

Every man's **money**: Not worth its price to everyone.
Works of art is not every man's **money**.

MORE

More is meant than meets the ear: Greater quantity.
In this article something **more** is meant than meets the ear.

More or less: About; in greater or less degree.
>They were **more** or less half dead when they
>arrived at the check-post.

MOUTH

Make **mouth** water: To have a strong desire for
something.
>The description of the sumptuous dishes to make
>our **mouths** water.

Stop the **mouth**: To silence someone.
>His forceful speech stopped the **mouth** of his
>opponents.

MOVE

Make a **move**: Go; start.
>It's getting late; we must make a **move** now.

On the **move**: Moving about.
>The soldiers are on the **move**.

MUSHROOM

Spring up like **mushroom**: To grow rapidly.
>Many small towns sprang up near Kolkata like
>**mushroom**.

N

NAIL

On the **nail**: Immediately.

Please distribute their wages on the **nail**.

Nail one's colour to the mast: To refuse to surrender, resist.

With a view to achieving success, they **nailed** their colours to the mast.

Hard as **nail**: In good physical condition.

The Gurkha soldiers are as hard as **nail**.

Nail to the counter: Expose as spurious.

As the statement was a downright lie I **nailed** it to the counter.

Right as **nails**: Perfectly right.

No politicians can be right as **nails**.

NAMBY-PAMBY

Namby-pamby: Weakly, sentimental, pretty but not exciting interest.

He hates to listen to his **namby**-pamby talk.

(He hates to talk to a **namby**-pamby girl.)

NAME

In the **name** of: For the sake of.

A good many persons have perished in the **name** of religion.

Take one's **name** off the books: To cease to be a member of.

The secretary took John's **name** off his books.

NAP

Caught **napping**: Caught unprepared.

Considering our defence preparedness, we can with reasonable certainty, say that no one will catch us **napping** in future.

NARROW

Narrow bed (home): Grave.

All the power and glory of a person will eventually lead him to his **narrow** bed.

Narrow circumstances: In poverty.

A man reared in **narrow** circumstances knows what poverty is actually like.

With **narrow** bounds: Of limited scope.

He could achieve limited success within **narrow** bounds.

NAY

Yes and **nay**: Shilly shally.

I can't get on well with yes and **nay** persons.

NEAR

Near and dear: Close, intimate.
However far we may wander, we cannot forget our **near** and dear.

NECESSITY

Of **necessity**: Forced to.
We, of **necessity**, had to live his house.

To make a virtue of **necessity**: To claim merit by doing disagreeable thing.
We are sometimes compelled to make a virtue of **necessity**.

Be under the **necessity** of: Compelled to do a thing for obvious reasons.
India is under the **necessity** of defending her neighbours from external aggression.

Necessity knows no law: Necessity knows no barriers.

NECK

Neck and crop: Completely.
Being furious with his servant, the manager turned him out **neck** and crop.

Neck and (by) **neck**: Equal; very close.
The new boy runs **neck** and (by) **neck** with George who usually tops the list.

Neck or nothing: Risking everything for success.
Climbing mountain is **neck** or nothing for mountaineers of all time and places.

<u>To break the **neck** of</u>: To complete the hardest part of the work.

>By the time my friend comes in the evening I will have done enough to break the **neck** of my day's hard work.

Neck <u>and heels</u>: Immediately.

>He was annoyed with his servant that he turned him out **neck** and heels.

NERVE

<u>Strain every **nerve**</u>: To try one's best.

>The people must strain every **nerve** to save their country from disintegration.

<u>A fit of **nerves**</u>: A disordered state of mind.

>I often see my uncle in a fit of **nerves**.

<u>Get on one's **nerves**</u>: Be a source of worry.

>It is his insolence that is getting on my **nerves**.

<u>Iron **nerves**</u>: Strength, vigour.

>Hitler was a man of iron **nerves**.

NEST

<u>It is an ill bird fouls its own **nest**</u>: Speaking ill of one's home.

NEW

New <u>fangled</u>: Newly achieved and despised.

>It is difficult to understand the **new** fangled ideas of our modern political upstarts.

New woman: Woman who prize freedom and rejects convention.

 After returning from U.K. she has totally become a **new** woman.

NEXT

Next to impossible: Almost impossible.

 The non-availability of funds made the execution of our plan **next** to impossible.

Next door to: Close to.

 It will be **next** door to being a coward if you behave in that manner.

Next to nothing: Almost nothing.

 If you squander your money like that very soon you will have **next** to nothing.

Her **next**: Husband.

 Her **next** was a business man.

NICETY

To a **nicety**: With great accuracy.

 The servant learnt the art of arranging flowers to a **nicety**.

A point of great **nicety**: Subtle distinction; unimportant.

 This is a point of great **nicety** which we need not discuss here now.

NICHE

To find a **niche** for oneself: Suitable condition.

 He found a **niche** for himself in business.

NICK

In the **nick** of time: Just in time.
    I went to see him in the **nick** of time.

NIGHT

Night and day: Always.
    I will think of you in my loneliness **night** and day.

Night of ignorance: Lacking knowledge.
    Our country is slowly coming out of the **night** of ignorance.

Nightmare: Dreadful experience.
    The long journey from Kolkata to Madras was a **nightmare**.

NINE

Nine day's wonder: Something that arouses interest for a time but is soon forgotten.
    They do not realize that the whole affair is a **nine** day's wonder.

NIP

Nip in the bud: To stop something at the early stage of progress.
    The landlord was fully aware of the peasants' hideous plot to kill him but he had the power to **nip** it in the bud.

NOSE

Lead by the **nose**: To make one follow blindly.
    The leader led his followers by the **nose**.

Poke one's **nose** into: To interfere with unnecessarily.
   You always seem to poke your **nose** into things
   which do not concern you in the least.

Under one's **nose**: Close to one.
   I am so much occupied with my work these days
   that I hardly notice what passes under my **nose**.

Turn up one's **nose**: To show disdain; dislike.
   The boy turned up his **nose** at the new pair of
   shoes.

To pay through the **nose**: To pay too much.
   I have a feeling that I have been paying him through
   the **nose** all these weeks for his eggs.

To bite (snap) one's **nose** off: To answer sharply.
   It is not unusual for a boss to bite off his **nose** to his
   subordinates.

Follow one's **nose**: Go straight.
   You cannot expect to rid yourself of different kinds
   of social involvements even if you follow your **nose**.

NOT

Not that: Not to be supposed that.
   Not that I wanted to hurt her feeling, but that she
   must know what place she occupies in the hearts of
   her own people.

Not by bread alone: Limited to satisfaction of physical
wants.
   Man does **not** live by bread alone.

NOTHING

Nothing less than: As much as.

I cannot say he is weak in sums, he scored **nothing** less than Peter, who is one of the best boys in his class.

Make **nothing** of: Treat as unimportant.

He made **nothing** of my promise.

Come to **nothing**: Turn out insignificant.

Since he does not exert himself much, our effort will surely come to **nothing**.

NOTICE

To take no **notice** of: Not to pay any attention to.

He took no **notice** of his brother's warning.

At short **notice**: In a short time.

He is unable to vacate the house at short **notice**.

NOW

Now that: Since now; seeing that.

Now that he has become a minister he will try to please everybody.

Now or never: This is the time.

The situation was extremely critical and **now** or never was the moment to declare the scheme.

NULL

Null and void: Useless; not binding.

Since Mr. Adam failed to keep his promise, the agreement became **null** and void.

NUT

<u>In a **nut**-shell</u>: In a few words.

He told us the story in a **nut**-shell.

Nuts <u>on</u>: Keen on.

It is not unusual for a teenager to be **nuts** on cricket.

<u>Off one's **nuts**</u>: Stupid; mad.

He drinks so much that he is usually found off his **nuts**.

NUTTY

Nutty <u>Upon</u>: Amorous; in love.

The manager is **nutty** upon his charming secretary.

O

OAR

Put in one's **oar**: To interfere.
  You have no right to put in your **oar** into our
  domestic troubles.

Rest (or Lie) on the **oared**: To rest.
  He has finished his studies now and is lying on his
  oars.

Chained to the **oar**: Compelled to do hard work.
  For the sake of his children he is chained to the **oar**.

Have an **oar** in everyman's boat: One who interferes;
meddler.
  Politicians have always an **oar** in everyman's boat.

OASIS

Oasis in a desert: Something which enlivens.
  A children's park is an **oasis** in a modern
  over-congested town.

OAT

Snow one's wild **oats**: To indulge in youthful follies.
  Modern youths despite repeated warnings, sow their
  wild **oats** only to face the disastrous consequences
  later.

OBJECT

Make an **objection** (take **objection** to): To object.
   Everybody will make an **objection** to this proposal
   of yours.

OBLIVION

Sink into **oblivion**: Be forgotten.
   Nehru's contribution for the restoration of human
   rights will never sink into **oblivion**.

OBSERVER

The observed of all **observers**: The center of attraction
cynosure.
   Miss Universe became the **observers** when she
   came to our town.

OBSESS

To be **obsessed** with: An idea that fills one's mind.
   The possibility of failure **obsessed** him.

OBEISANCE

To make **obeisance**: To bow down as a mark of
respect.
   If you make **obeisance** to the king, you are not
   liable to be punished for misdemeanor.

OCCASION

Have **occasion**: To have some business.
   I had **occasion** to see my ailing friend during my
   short visit to Kolkata.

<u>Take **occasion**</u>: To take advantage of an opportunity.
    The boy took **occasion** to meet his parents during
    the winter holidays.

<u>Give **occasion** to</u>: To cause.
    His success has **occasioned** much happiness.

ODD

<u>**Odds** with</u>: At variance with.
    He is at **odds** with his fellowmen.

<u>Against heavy **odds**</u>: Against heavy circumstances.
    The Indians did well in the last cricket match held
    in England even though they had to play against
    heavy **odds**.

<u>By long **odds**</u>: By a big margin; decidedly.
    Pinky is by long **odds** the best girl in the class.

<u>**Odds**</u>: Balance of advantage or conditions.
    The **odds** are in our favour.

<u>**Odd**-come-short</u>: Remnant; left-over.
    Since you came last, you can satisfy with
    odd-come-short.

ODOUR

<u>Be in bad **odour**</u>: To have a bad reputation.
    The Negroes after the war are in very bad **odour** in
    the United States.

OFF

<u>**Off** and on</u>: Occasionally.
  I go to his place **off** and on.

<u>Show **off**</u>: To make a display.
  It is his habit to show **off**.

<u>Well **off**</u>: To be in congenial circumstances.
  He is financially well **off**.

OFFENCE

<u>Give **offence**</u>: To hurt feelings.
  See that you don't give **offence** to anyone.

<u>Take **offence**</u>: To be offended.
  They took **offence** at what I said.

<u>Take the **offensive**</u>: Aggressive.
  The Germans were in a position to take the
  offensive before the war.

OFFICE

<u>Perform the last **office**</u>: To perform rites for the dead.
  We performed the last **offices** for the old man who
  had died in an accident.

OFFING

<u>In the **offing**</u>: Coming shortly.
  Everybody thinks that another devaluation of the
  rupee is in the **offing**.

OIL

<u>Burn midnight **oil**</u>: To work far into the night.
   When the examination approaches near, it is not
   unusual for students to burn midnight **oil**.

<u>Pour **oil** on the waters</u>: To quite a disturbed situation.
   India is pouring **oil** on the African waters.

<u>Pour **oil** into the fire</u>: Aggravate or to make the matter
worse.

<u>Strike **oil**</u>: To find oil through boring; to succeed.
   The Russian experts struck **oil** in a place near
   Mumbai.
   He struck **oil** in his business.

Oil <u>one's palms</u>: To bribe.
   The dismal spectacle to-day is that no one can
   get anything done without **oiling** the palms of the
   persons in power.

OLD

Old <u>as hills</u>: Very ancient.
   There is nothing new in their religious ceremonies;
   What you have witnessed is as **old** as the hills.

Old <u>and young</u>: Everyone.
   Old and young were present in the meeting.

Old <u>head on the young shoulders</u>: wisdom beyond.
   This glorious child carries an **old** head on young
   shoulders.

Old woman: Fussy and timid.
Don't behave like an **old** woman.

Old man of the sea: A man of resolute determination.
Nehru has been regarded by his compatriots as an **old** man of the sea.

Old bird: Very shrewd; experienced.
He is an **old** bird and cannot be caught so easily.

OLIVE

To hold out the **olive** branch: To show gestures for reconciliation.
The people of North Viet Nam will never hold out the **olive** branch before the imperialists.

OMELETTE

Cannot make an **omelette** without breaking eggs: End necessitates means.

OMISSION

Omissions and **commissions**: Negative and positive mistakes.
Not by any manner of means I can excuse your **omissions** and **commissions**.

ON

On and **on**: Continuously.
They rode **on** and **on** till they came to a rest house.

On and alert: Watchful.
After Chinese attack all of us are now **on** the alert.

On time: Punctual.

The players arrived here yesterday **on** time.

ONCE

All at **once**: All of a sudden.

His behaviour changed all at **once**.

Once and again: More than once.

I told **once** and again not to disturb me while I am studying.

Once in a while: Rarely.

Accident like this takes place only **once** in a while.

Once for all: Finally.

I want you to sign an English song **once** for all.

ONE

At **one**: In agreement.

Here I am at **one** with you.

All **one**: Of no importance.

Go wherever you like; it is all **one** to me.

One or the other: This or that.

You can choose **one** or the other.

One and all: Everybody with no exception.

The national hero received a warm welcome from **one** and all.

OPEN

<u>In the **open** air</u>: Out of doors.

We slept in the **open** air and passed the oppressive night.

<u>With **open** arms</u>: Gladly,

The received us with **open** arms.

<u>**Open** one's eyes</u>: To begin to perceive the truth; to realise the true state of affairs.

The disastrous consequence of racial violence **opened** the eyes of every citizen of India.

OPINION

<u>Good **opinion**</u>: Good impression.

He has a very good **opinion** of his servant.

<u>No two **opinions**</u>: No difference of opinions.

There can be no two **opinions** about his truthfulness.

OPPORTUNITY

<u>Let slip an **opportunity**</u>: To miss a chance.

See that you do not let any **opportunity** slip from your hand.

<u>Embrace (or seize) an **opportunity**</u>: To avail oneself of a chance.

He embraced (or seized) the **opportunity** of striking him with a stick.

ORDER

In **order**: Fit condition.
> Put your clothes in **order**.

In **order** to: With a view to.
> He left no stone unturned in **order** to save his brother from his enemies.

I n the **order** of: Order of succession.
> All the names were put down in the alphabetical **order**.

Order of the day: Prevailing fashion.
> Frugality in everything is the **order** of the day.

Out of **order**: Not in good condition.
> My car is out of **order**.

Set one's house in **order**: To regulate one's house properly.
> If you want others to learn from you, you should set your house in **order** first.

Order: A badage of honour.
> He wore all his **orders** on the occasion of the Independence Day.

To take **orders**: To be clergyman.
> He took **orders** from the Pope in his young age.

Of high **order**: Of good quality.
> They have printed a book of very high **order**.

To take **order**: To take appropriate measures.
You can take **order** to put an end to his cruel deeds.

OUT

Out and **out**: Completely.
Napoleon was **out** and **out** a dictator.

Out and away: By far.
She is **out** and away the best girl in her class.

Out for: **Out** to do.
They are **out** for mischief.

Be **out**: Away from; to appear.
His brother is **out**.
The stars are all **out** to-night.

Out of: From; beyond.
You cannot make anything **out** of nothing.
It is **out** of his power to refuse the terms.

Times **out** of number: Many times; countless.
I have warned him times **out** of number to refrain
from such anti-social activities.

Out of date: Obsolete; old-fashion.
The book is **out** of date.

Out of the wood: Out of danger.
It seems that we are still not **out** of the wood.

Out of tune: In bad temper.
Because of his mental worries he is mostly **out** of tune.

OVER

Over and above: In addition to.
I gave him some money **over** and above the amount he had already received from his parents.

Over against: Opposite.
There is a temple **over** against our school.

Over and over: Repeatedly.
He recited the poem **over** and **over**.

To **over** shoot oneself: To exaggerate.
When he starts talking about football, he usually **over** shoots himself.

OWE

To owe one a grudge: To cherish a resentment against.

Owing to: Because of.
The match was cancelled **owing** to bad weather.

Have one's **own** way: To do as one wishes.
Let him have his **own** way.

P

Mind your **P's** and Q's: Take care of what you say and do.

>   You can get on well with your men if you only mind your **P's** and Q's.

Put a person through his **paces**: Test one's abilities in action.

>   It seems that our government does not put our aspiring diplomats through their **paces** before they are finally absorbed in foreign services.

Keep **pace** with: To keep uo with.

>   He has been striving very hard to keep **pace** with the class.

Go the **pace**: To indulge in vicious living.

>   You cannot at the present moment afford to go the **pace** as others are doing, else you will repent afterwards.

At a snail's **pace**: Very slowly, completely exhausted.

>   After a day's hard work, the farmer walked toward his home at a snail's **pace**.

PACK

A **pack** of lies: Downright lies.

>   What he said was a **pack** of lies.

Pack off: To dismiss.

    I **packed** all my servants off.

Packed with: Filled with.

    His head is **packed** with all stupid ideas which can hardly be translated into action.

PADDLE

Paddle one's own canoe: To be self dependant mind one's own business.

    One should learn to be self-reliant by **paddling** one's own canoe.

PAIN

Take **pains**: To be careful, to make effort.

    He has taken great **pains** to go through the answer papers.

PAINT

To **paint** the town red: To cause commotion.

    The outlaw **painted** the town red yesterday.

Paint out: Efface with paint.

    The unnecessary slogan will soon be **painted** out from the poster-wall.

Not so black as she is **painted**: Represented.

    You can rest assured that she is not so black as she is **painted**.

PALE

Pale into insignificance: To appear less important.
Beside Nehru's the achievement of all his contemporaries **pale** into insignificance.

Within the **pale**: Within the boundary.
Our village falls within the **pale** of restricted area.

Beyond the **pale**: Outside the boundary.
They constructed a house beyond the **pale** of the town.

PALM

Bear the **palm**: To bag prizes.
He bore the **palm** in the Annual Sports of his school.

Give the **palm to**: To recognize the superiority of.
After having studied their views, he gave the **palm** to English education.

Palm off: To pass by fraud.
He tried his best to **palm** off a second-hand car on me but luckily I avoided on some pretexts.

Palm days: Prosperous days.
He in his **palmy** days could never of his friends who stood in the dark days of his life.

PAN

Pan out: To succeed.
His scheme is **panning** out well.

PAPER

Commit to paper: Write.

He has committed all his ideas to **paper**.

Put pen to **paper**: Start writing.

He has simply to put his pen to **paper** and the thoughts just flow.

Paper profits: Hypothetical gains.

There is bound to be a big difference between the **paper** profits and the real gain later.

On **paper**: Outwardly; judged from figures.

On **paper** India has made a tremendous progress in every field of activity.

Send in one's **papers**: Resign.

He has sent in his **papers** to the manager after careful deliberation.

Paper tiger: Causing false fear.

America and China consider each other to be **paper** tigers.

Paper war: War carried on through books and newspapers.

Paper was sometimes paves the way for real war.

PAR

At **par** or On a **par** with: On a level with.

He is on a **par** with the best boy of his class.

Below **par**: Below the official price; average.
   Rich is being sold below **par** in the open market.

Par excellence: That excels in quality.
   Shakespeare is a playwright **par** excellence.

PARADE

Make a **parade** of: Pompous display.
   A great man never makes a **parade** of his deeds.

PARADISE

Earthly paradise: Heaven.
   History bears ample testimony that our country was
   once an **earthly** paradise.

PARLEY

Hold a **parley** with: To discuss.
   The rival parties are holding a **parley** on peace
   terms.

PART

Man of **parts**: Talented; accomplishment.
   Nehru was a man of **parts**.

In good **part**: favourably.
   No matter however sour your advice may be, he
   takes it in good **part**.

In **part**: Partly.
   I agree with you in **part**.

Part <u>with</u>: Separate.

He has no other alternatives but to **part** with his belongings.

<u>Take</u> **part** <u>in</u>: To share.

They could not take **part** in out national festival.

<u>For the most</u> **part**: Mostly.

For the most **part**, the black marketeers can have been able to escape punishments so easily.

<u>For (on) my</u> **part**: As far as it concerns me.

For (on) my **part** I have not the slightest doubt of his ability.

Part <u>and parcel of</u>: Essential portion.

This house has become a **part** and parcel of my life.

<u>To do (play) one's</u> **part**: Do one's duty.

Do your **part** well and the matter ends there.

<u>Have neither</u> **part** <u>nor lot in</u>: To have no concern in.

I have neither **part** nor lot in their struggle for power.

PARTICULAR

In **particular**: Specially.

Cho, in **particular**, was impressed by his speech.

PARTY

<u>Be a</u> **party** <u>to</u>: To take part in.

He is liable to be punished for he was a **party** to the crime.

PASS

Pass by: (a) To go near. (b) To take no notice of.

   (a) While **passing** by his house yesterday, I saw his beautiful garden.

   (b) We need not go through his manuscript minutely; some irrelevant portions can be **passed** by.

Pass for: To be regarded as.

   He **passes** for a good sportsman.

Pass off: (a) To become less intense (b) To pretend.

   (a) The storm is gradually **passing** off.

   (b) He **passes** off to be an experts in politics.

Pass through: (a) To travel through. (b) To undergo.

   (a) If you travel to Goa by train from Kolkata, you will **pass** through many a tunnel.

   (b) The country is **passing** through a very critical time.

Pass on: To go on.

   Let us **pass** on to the next item of the agenda.

Pass over: To over look.

   This chapter of the book being an important one, you cannot easily **pass** over.

Pass away: To disappear, to die.

   The dark day have **passed** away.

   His brother **passed** away in the hospital to-day.

Come to **pass**: To take place.
A great many things have come to **pass** after the death of our beloved leader Nehru.

Passion for: Ardent desire.
He has a **passion** for writing short stories.

PASSPORT

Passport: Something that clears the way to success.
Industry has become a real **passport** to success in any field of activity.

PAT

Pat on the back: To strike gently, approval.
I **patted** him on his back for having topped the list in his class.

PATCH

Patch up: To mend.
We must **patch** up our minor differences amicably.

Not a **patch** on: Not fit to be compared.
He is not a **patch** on you for intelligence.

PAVE

Paved with: Filled with.
The road to his house was **paved** with beautiful flowering trees.

Pavement artist: One who draws on the pavement.
We do not have many **pavement** artist in India.

Pave the way for: To prepare for.
Hard work **paved** the way for his final success in the examination.

PAY

Pay court to: To flatter.
He cannot be expected to **pay** court to the people just to win their votes.

Pay off: To pay and discharge a worker.
The owner **paid** his driver off.

Pay a visit: To go to see a person.
I must **pay** a visit to your place one of these days.

Pay for: To make amends for; to bear the cost of.
He had to **pay** for his mistakes in full measure.
Sikkim's defence is India's concerns and shoe does not have to **pay** for it.

Pay one back in one's own coin: To take revenge; tit for tat.
If he has betrayed you twice, you are at your liberty to **pay** him back in his own coin.

Pay one's way: To live free from debt.
He is not rich but can **pay** his own way.

Pay one's score: To settle one's accounts.
He was so poor that he failed to **pay** his score at the time of his death.

<u>**Pay** the piper</u>: To pay cost.
    The U.S.A. has solely been **paying** the piper for war in Vietnam.

<u>In the **pay** of</u>: In the employment.
    So long as they are in the **pay** of the government they cannot actively take part in politics.

PEACE

<u>Hold one's **peace**</u>: To be silent.
    They were yelling at each other but held their **peace** when the police inspector appeared in the scene.

<u>Keep the **peace**</u>: To refrain from breaking the peace.
    If we fail to keep the **peace** in our country we will only be inviting troubles from outside.

<u>**Peace** at any price</u>: Peace under all conditions.
    We must strive for **peace** at any price, else we will not be able to tackle our problems under the prevailing atmosphere of cold war.

<u>Make **peace** with</u>: To have friendly relations with.
    India has made **peace** with her neighbour.

PEAK

<u>At the **peak** of</u>: The highest point.
    She is at the **peak** of her success.

PEARL

To cast **pearls** before swine: To give something to one who does not know its worth.

Reading religious books before them is casting **pearls** before swine.

PECK

Peck of worries: Large amount of worries.

He is having a **peck** of worries at present.

PEEP

Peep of dawn: First appearance.

I am usually off my bed before the birds start chirping at the **peep** of dawn.

PEER

To **peer** at: To look carefully.

He was **peering** at himself in the new mirror of his dressing room.

PEG

To **peg** away: To keep on.

We wanted him to **peg** away at his new job.

To take a person down a **peg** or two: To humble or to pull down.

It is his bad habit to take any person down a **peg** or two.

PEN

Wields a vigorous **pen**: To be able to write forcefully.

Nehru wields a vigorous **pen**.

PENDULUM

Swing of the **pendulum**: Alteration of power in politics.
  A swing of **pendulum** transforms many an
  intellectual pigmy into a political giant.

PENNY

A pretty **penny**: A considerable sum of money.
  It cost me a pretty **penny** for this house.

Penny wise and pound foolish: Wise in small profits but
wasteful in large ones.
  No sensible man can afford to be **penny** wise and
  pound foolish in his dealing with other people.

Take care of the **pence** and pound will take care
of itself: Small saving today will turn into a big sum
tomorrow.

PERIL

At one's **peril**: At the risk of loss or injury.
  If you want to swim in the deep end of the river, you
  can do so at your own **peril**.

PETARD

Hoist with one's own **petard**: caught in one's own trap.
  The enemies were hoist with their own **petard**.

PICK

Pick of the basket: The best of anything.
  The radiogram I bought yesterday was undoubtedly
  the **pick** of the basket.

Pick and choose: To carefully select.
She bores anyone by her **pick** and choose shopping.

Pick up: To recover from illness.
He is **picking** up from his recent illness.

Pick one's way: To walk carefully.
He is **picking** his way with utmost care through the slimy path.

PIECE

Piece by piece: Bit by bit.
He finished telling the long story to his children piece by **piece**.

Of a **piece**: Of the same sort.
He is of a **piece** with that fool.

PIG

Bring one's **pig to a pretty market**: To make a bad bargain in any venture.
He realised a bit too late that in this particular business he had brought his **pigs** to a pretty market.

PILL

A bitter **pill**: To endure something unpleasant.
The teacher's remark proved to be too bitter a **pill** for the child to swallow.

PIN

Pin one's faith: To trust.
> Great men usually **pin** their faith on their own conscience.

Pin down: To hold a person to his promise.
> He cannot betray us; we will **pin** him down to the agreement.

PINCH

At a **pinch**: At times of need.
> He is always ready to help his friend at a **pinch**.

To feel the **pinch** of: Painful experience.
> It was actually last year or so that the Indians felt the **pinch** of famine.

PITCH

Pitch into: To fall headlong; to attack.
> The fox **pitched** into the ditch.

Pitch on: To decide; select.
> They **pitched** on a nice plan but failed to execute it owing to paucity of funds.

Little **pitchers** have long ears: The children are apt to overhear.

PLACE

Give **place** to: To make room for.
> He being a medicore player had to give **place** to a superior one.

Out of **place**: Not suitable.

The remark that you made yesterday about one of the members of the committee was rather unpleasant and out of **place**.

In **place** of: Instead of.

A new boy was appointed monitor in **place** of a girl.

To take place: To happen.

Many revolutionary changes had taken **place** in India since 1947.

PLAY

To **play** fast and loose: To be inconsistent.

Having so often **played** fast and loose with them in the past she sank low in their eyes.

Play second fiddle to: To act as a subordinate.

A naughty person like him cannot **play** second fiddle to anybody.

Play upon: To deceive.

Movies **play** upon our minds in a slow but sure manner.

Play off: To set one against the other.

She derived immense pleasure in **playing** off one against the other.

Play upon words: To use words in such a way as to convey double meanings.

Do you mean to impose him by thus **playing** upon words?

PLEA

On the **plea** of: On the grounds of.

He has requested for an extension of his leave on the **plea** of ill-health.

PLEDGE

To redeem one's **pledge**: To fulfill one's promises.

When I have told you I will help you, I am determined to redeem my **pledge**

PLUCK

Pluck out: To pull out.

He **plucked** all the weeds out from his garden.

Pluck up courage (or one's spirit): To have courage.

He **plucked** all his courage to face the trials and tribulations of life.

PLUME

To **plum** oneself on: To take pride in.

He **plumed** himself on his high academic achievements.

Borrowed **plumes** (or feathers): False colours.

Sensible persons rarely appear in borrowed **plumes**.

PLY

To **ply** with gold: To bribe with gold

Politician in power to-day, if **plied** with gold, is capable of doing incredible things.

POCKET

Pocket an insult: To put up with it without protest.
  He had to **pocket** an insult for his guilt.

Out of **pocket**: To lose money in a deal.
  He turned a pauper when he was out of **pocket** in his business.

To have someone in one's **pocket**: Under complete control of.
  The black marketeers normally keep the custodians of law and order in their **pocket**.

POINT

Point blank: In a straight-forward manner.
  I am not scared of his position; I will tell him everything **point** blank.

The turning **point**: A definite time at which a great change takes place.
  The prince stayed with the priest only for a short time but nevertheless it proved to be a turning **point** in his career.

The crowing **point**: Highest point.
  Sastriji reached the crowing **point** of his glory at Tashkent.

Make a **point** of: To consider as essential.
  He always makes a **point** of placing some sort of barriers to my proposals.

On the **point** of: On the brink of.
　　He was on the **point** of death when the doctor
　　came.

POP

To **pop** the question: To propose marriage.
　　It is high time that you **pop** the question to her.

POT

Go to **pot**: To be ruined.
　　There is every possibility that his business will go
　　to **pot**.
　　The **pots** call the kettle black: Used when a person
　　blames another for faults he too is not free from.

Keep the **pot** boiling: To earn enough for fool and drink.
　　He does not get enough to keep the **pot** boiling.

POWDER

Not worth **powder** and shot: Not worth the trouble.
　　Fishing in this river is not worth **powder** and shot.

Keep the **powder** dry: To be ready for any eventuality.
　　The rebel leader told his followers to keep their
　　powder dry.

PRECEDENT

Set a **precedent**: To establish a rule.
　　By allowing that boy to escape without punishment
　　the teacher set a bad **precedent**.

PRECEDENCE

To take **precedence** over: Right to a great place of importance.

It is not very unusual for an army officer to take **precedence** over a soldier.

PREFERENCE

In **preference** to: To consider one as more desirable.

I might choose a radiogram in **preference** to that of a car as a gift to my wife.

PREJUDICE

To the **prejudice** of: Detrimental to the interest of.

Our government has not done anything to the **prejudice** of the muslims living in India.

Prejudice one's against: To influence one's mind against another.

She has **prejudiced** her sister against me.

PREMIUM

At a **premium**: In demand; obtained at an increased value.

Dark-green jades are sold at a **premium**.

Put a **premium** on: To increase the value of.

By putting a **premium** on science education a step has been taken toward technology advancement.

PRESS

To **press** for: To demand.

The factory workers **pressed** for the fulfillment of their demands.

To be hard **pressed**: To be in great difficulty.
> When he was hard **pressed** I tried my best to get him out of the rut.

Liberty of the **press**: Right to publish divergent views without government's interference.
> There is no liberty of the **press** in a dictatorial regime.

PRETEXT

Under **pretext** (pretence) of: On the plea of.
> He failed to extend his leave under **pretext** of illness.

To make **pretence** to: False show.
> He detests the idea of making **pretence** to his wealth.

PREVAIL

Prevail on: To persuade.
> I **prevailed** on him to see the picture with me.

Prevail against (over): To gain triumph.
> Virtue will in the long run **prevail** over vices.

PREY

Prey upon: To kill; plunder or worry.
> The sudden illness of his wife **preyed** upon his mind.

PRICE

Beyond **price**: Priceless.
> Honour is beyond **price**.

Set a **price** on one's head: To offer a reward for capturing (or putting to death) a person.

> The Government has set a **price** on the head of the rebel leader.

PRICK

Prick up one's ears: To listen attentively.

> You must **prick** up your ears when the professor dwells on some important topics.

PRINCE

Hamlet without the **Prince** of Denmark: Something robbed of its brilliance.

> The history of modern India without Nehru is a Hamlet without the **Prince** of Denmark.

PRINCIPLE

On **Principle**: According to certain fixed rule of action.

> On **principle** I refused to drink.

PROBE

To **probe**: To carefully examine.

> People demanded that Government should **probe** the conduct of some Chinese officials of the Embassy.

PROOF

To stand the **proof**: To face the trial.

> He stood the **proof** to the entire satisfaction of his adversaries.
>
> The **proof** the pudding is in the eating: Practice is the acid test of theory.

PROS

Pros and cons: Argument for and against.

After carefully studying the **pros** and cons of the subject I have taken this final step.

PUFF

Puffed off: Swollen with pride.

He has to talk to a **puffed** off person.

PULL

To **pull** on: To live.

He is **pulling** on well with his new servant.

Pull a face: To twist a face.

He **pulled** a face when his professor passed an unhappy remark about his rudeness.

To **pull** down: Weak; to demolish.

He looks a bit **pull** down.

They **pulled** down the house in no time.

To **pull** up: Checked.

He was **pulled** up by his father for telling lies.

Pull wires (or strings): To act secretly.

As there was so much of wire **pulling** that he does not know what the result will be like.

Pull in: To check.

He is awfully wasteful and, must **pull** in else he will have to face the music.

To **pull** through: To recover.
  In about a month's time the patient will surely **pull** through.

Pull off: To manage anything successfully.
  He has been **pulling** off his uncle's business for a number of years.

Pull one's weight: To do one's share.
  I can't say he hasn't **pulled** his weight to help his starving relatives.

Pull to pieces: Tear; criticice.
  He will **pull** you to pieces in a fit of furry.

Pull about: To treat roughly.
  He was **pulled** about in the presence of his friends.

PULP

To reduce to **pulp**: To crush.
  The robber was reduced to **pulp** at the hands of the villagers.

PULSE

Feel one's **pulse**: To understand one's mind.
  I merely said that to feel ones **pulse**.

PURCHASE

His life is not worth an hour's **purchase**: He cannot be trusted to last an hour.

PURPOSE

On **purpose**: Intentionally.
   I did it on **purpose**.

In **purpose**: Determination.
   He does not lack in **purpose**.

Serve the **purpose**: To meet the requirements.
   This pen will serve my **purpose**.

PURSE

Hold the **purse** strings: To have complete control over expenditure.
   There is hardly any hope of getting any money because they hold the **purse** strings.

PUSH

Push off: To move away.
   The passengers on board ship **pushed** off from their native shores.

Pushed for: Hard pressed.
   He is **pushed** for money.

Push down: (i) To overthrow, (ii) To demote.
   (i) He drove so recklessly that he **pushed** down an old man.
   (ii) The officer was **pushed** down for his mortal lapses.

Push on: To move forward.
   The soldiers **pushed** on.

Push through: To bring to a conclusion.
We should not waste time in **pushing** this matter
through.

Push oneself through: To press forward.
It was quite a difficult task to **push** myself through
the crowd.

PUT

Put up: (i) To lodge, (ii) To store away, (iii) To offer for
sale.
(i) He is **putting** up in a luxurious hotel.
(ii) The gold ornaments so far collected for defence
should be **put** in the Government treasury.
(iii) The shopkeeper **put** up a nice dancing doll in
his show-case.

Put up with: To endure patiently.
The pain was too much and he could not **put** up
with it.

Put about: To put to inconvenience.
As they did not offer him a good quarter first, he was
put about for a good deal of time.

Put away: To renounce; give up.
You must **put** away these bad habits of yours.

Put by: Store up.
He is so extravagant that he has not **put** by any
money for the future.

Put back: To delay or hinder.
    The patient's progress has been **put** back by the
    carelessness of the hospital staff.

Put down: To suppress; to attribute.
    The Premier was determined to **put** down
    lawlessness in the country.
    The success he achieved can safely be **put** down to
    his painstaking labour.

Put forth: To shoot out.
    The oppressive heat made all the green leaves
    lifeless which the trees had **put** forth in the spring.

Put off: To lay aside; to baffle; to postpone.
    Put off your coat.
    As he is a good football-player, you cannot **put** him
    off by any tricky movement of your body.
    Never **put** off till tomorrow what you can do today.

Put on: To clothe oneself; to assume; to behave
proudly.
    Put on your shirt properly.
    Nobody likes him because he always tries to **put**
    on airs.

Put out: free from; to extinguish.
    The injection **put** the patient out of danger.
    Please **put** out the light before you go to bed.

Put forward: To set forth.
    The questions that he has **put** forward in his report
    defies all solutions.

Put through: To accomplish.
He has successful **put** through a piece of work which he was entrusted with.

Put over: To place in command; to do something successfully.
The manager decided to **put** his assistant over to his place.
The task is difficult but he will **put** it over.

Put in: To present in a formal manner; to spend.
Don't be in a hurry to **put** in your application now.
I have **put** in seventeen years of service in this firm.

To **put** to: To cause to happen.
He apologised for having **put** him to inconvenience.

Q

Quack

Quack rem dies: Ignorant devices.
The maladies of your nation cannot be cured by **quack** remedies.

QUAGMIRE

In the **quagmire**: In difficulties.
It is fortunate that politics threw him in the **quagmire**.

QUAIL

Quail-call: Whistle for luring someone.
It was his **quail**-call that I listened to every morning.

QUALIFICATION

Hedged with **qualification**: Vague but well guarded.
The opposition leader's statement was hedged with **qualifications**.

QUANDARY

To be in a **quandary**: To be in a state of uncertainty.
After the last unsuccessful war the Arabs are in a **quandary**.

QUANTITY

<u>Negligible **quantity**</u>: A person that need not be reckoned with.

They being all big politicians, he found himself a negligible **quantity** there.

QUARREL

<u>Find **quarrel** in a straw</u>: Given to fault finding.

He has a nasty habit of finding **quarrel** in a straw.

<u>To **quarrel** with one's bread and butter</u>: To act in such a way as to lose one's means of subsistence.

Do your duty well and you will never have to **quarrel** with your bread and butter.

QUARTER

<u>To give no **quarter**</u>: Not to give any shelter.

The government decided to give no **quarter** to the fugitives from China.

<u>From all **quarters**</u>: From all parts of the world.

Students come to Oxford from all **quarters**.

QUEER

<u>**Queer** fish</u>: An eccentric person.

He is a **queer** fish.

<u>**Queer** to pitch</u>: To spoil another's affair purposely.

If he comes to know what we are doing here, he will definitely try to **queer** a pitch.

In **queer** street: To be in trouble; debt or disrepute.
> Behave yourself well else you will land up yourself
> in the **queer** street.

QUEST

In **quest** of: In search of.
> Buddha moved from place to place in **quest** of
> salvation.

QUESTION

Beyond (out of) **question**: Beyond all doubt;
impracticable.
> His ability is beyond **question**.

Call in **question**: To challenge.
> The validity of his remarks was called in **question**.

Vexed **question**: Intricate question.
> We surely do not want to go into the vexed
> **questions** of national language and the medium of
> instruction in schools.

Out of **question**: Not worth discussing; impracticable.
> I know Biswas's brother well and any reflection on
> his conduct is out of **question**.

Beg the **question**: To avoid the real argument.
> If you say that family planning has been very
> successful in India you are only begging the
> **question**.

QUEUE

To **queue** up: To wait in a line.

I had to **queue** up for a seat in the bus.

QUICK

To the **quick**: (1) Through and through, (2) Tender flesh below the nails.

(1) He is communist to the **quick**.

(2) He has a nasty habit of biting his nails to the **quick**.

QUIET

To have a **quiet** dig: To taunt someone mildly.

She had a **quiet** dig at the professor.

On the **quiet**: Secretly.

He does his work on the **quiet**.

QUIT

Be **quits**: To be even with one.

As far as education is concerned he tried his utmost to be **quits** with his fellows.

To **quit** oneself well: To behave nicely.

Everybody likes him because he **quits** himself well.

QUITE

Quite to one's taste: Suited to one's taste.

Don't worry, I will send things **quite** to your taste.

R

The three **R's**: Reading, writing and arithmetic.
First of all the farmers were taught the three **R's** in the adult education centre.

RABID

Rabid socialist: Enthusiastic; fanatical socialist.
The member of **rabid** socialist is increasing very fast.

RACK

Go **rack** and ruin: To go to destruction.
It is because of the black marketeers that the country is going to **rack** and ruin.

On the **rack**: To be tortured.
I have been on the **rack** to find a way out of this impasse.

RACKET

Be on the **racket**: To indulge in merry making.
Be off on the **racket** for so many days is really amazing that you should.

Racy speech: Spirited.
He made a **racy** speech in the parliament.

RADICAL

Radical humour: Natural humour.
> You can ill-afford to miss some **radical** humour contained in his book.

The **radical** rottenness of human nature: Inherent human drawbacks.
> Selfishness is the **radical** rottenness of human nature.

Radical change, reform, cure: Affecting the foundation or going to the root.
> What we badly require is a **radical** cure to our many social evils.

RAG

In **rags**: In tattered clothes.
> The boy was in **rags**.

Cooked **rags**: To cook till it falls to pieces.
> He cooked the meat to **rags**.

Not a **rag** of evidence: To find no evidence.
> Not a **rag** of evidence he could give to support his allegations.

Flying **rags** of clouds: irregular pieces of clouds.
> Immediately after the rains, we could see flying **rags** of clouds atop hill.

RAIL

Rail at: To scold.

The parents always **railed** at their children for their idleness.

Off the **rails**: Disorder.
It is poverty that drives people off the **rails**.

RAIN

Rain cats and dogs: A heavy shower.
It has been **raining** cats and dogs for the last few days.

Rain or shine: In good or bad weather.
Rain or shine, I will be coming to your house tomorrow.

A **rain** day: A time of need.
He had saved enough against the **rain** day.

RAISE

To **raise** the wind: To obtain money.
We are trying our best to **raise** the wind for the education of the deprived children.

To **raise** a question: To bring up for consideration.
It will be futile to **raise** the question of price freeze without giving due consideration to wage freeze first.

Raise a siege: To give up the attempt.
The Army forced the enemies to **raise** siege of Kashmir.

To **raise** a laugh: To cause laughter.
  His witty jokes **raised** a laugh.

To **raise** eyebrows: Sign of disdain.
  He **raised** the eyebrows at my new suit.

To **raise** the country: To arouse or excite.
  Tilak **raised** the country with his fiery speech.

Raise one from one's knees: To elevate to a higher position.
  Nehru **raised** a many countries in Asia from their knees.

Raise a storm: To create a commotion.
  Some opposition members **raised** a storm in the Parliament on the issue of language.

RAKE

Rake up: To revive.
  Forget those unpleasant things. It is no use **raking** up the past.

Rake out: To search carefully.
  He tried to **rake** out secrets from the prisoners.

RANDOM

At **random**: Haphazard.
  You cannot rely on his words; he talks at **random**.

RANGE

To **range** with: To join.
>Students should under no circumstances **range** with the politicians.

RANK

Rank and file: Common soldiers; private.
>When a battle is won the work of the **rank** and file is often forgotten.

To **rank** high: To have a high place or position.
>Among philosophers of international repute Radha-krishna **ranks** very high.

Rankle in the mind (or heart): To be a source of pain.
>The fact that he married at a very young age still **rankles** in his mind.

RANSOM

King's **ransom**: A large sum of money.
>It cost me a king's **ransom** to build this house.

Hold one to **ransom**: To detain a person with a view to obtaining money at the time of his release.

RAP

Rap on the knuckles: Reproof.
>For his rudeness he got a **rap** on the knuckles from his brother.

Rap and rend: To plunder.
>Bahadur Shah came to India merely to **rap** and rend.

Rapt attention: Whole-hearted attention.
The children listened to his talk with **rapt** attention.

To go into **rapture**: To find great delight in.
He went into **rapture** over his dramatic speech.

RAT

Smell a **rat**: To have suspicion.
I smell a **rat** in their secret meeting.

RATE

At any **rate**: In any case, by any means.
He will, at any **rate**, have to play his game.

RATHER

Would (Had) **rather**: Prefer to.
I would (had) **rather** go than stay.

RATTLE

Rattle the saber: Threaten war.
The enemies have started **rattling** their sabers but we are least frightened.

RAW

Touch one on the **raw**: To hurt one's feelings.
The old woman burst into tears when her son touched her on the **raw**.

READ

Read a lesson: To admonish.
His father **read** him a fine lesson.

Read into the words: To find more meanings than is intended by the author.

He always **reads** too much into the words.

Read between the lines: To discover a meaning that are not expressed.

The professor told his students to **read** Nehru's writings between the lines.

REAP

To **reap** the fruits of: To enjoy the consequences of.

He is **reaping** the fruits of his labour.

To **reap** when one has not sown: To enjoy fruits of other's labour.

Some people are fortunate enough to **reap** where they have not sown.

To sow wind and **reap** whirlwind: To suffer the consequences of ones misdeeds.

If you risk too much in a business you will sow wind and **reap** whirlwind.

REAR

In the **rear**: Behind.

There were still a few weary travellers coming far in the **rear**.

To bring up the **rear**: To come last; to follow.

Josephin is a weakling and in matters of sports she always brings up the **rear**.

Hang on the **rear** of: To follow with the view of attacking.
  Modi being the author of all these troubles the
  policemen are hanging on his **rear**.

Take enemy in the **rear**: To attack from behind.
  They made all preparation to take the enemy in
  the **rear**.

REASON

Stands to **reason**: Generally admitted.
  What he said yesterday stands to **reason**.

Without rhyme or **reason**: Without any cause.
  His expelled his open without rhyme or **reason**.

By **reason** of: On account of.
  By **reason** of his prolonged illness he could not fare
  any better in his last examination.

In all **reason**: For the sake of justice.
  This is my order and you must in all **reason**, carry it
  out.

RECKON

Reckon on: To depend.
  I am your friend and you can always **reckon** on me.

Reckon with: To settle accounts with.
  I have got many things to **reckon** with him.

RECOIL

Recoil from: To be frightened.

Whenever he thinks of that dreadful dream his mind **recoils** with fear.

RECORD

On **record**: Preserved in writing.

The statement he made in the court is on **record**.

Keep to the **record**: Stick to the relevant.

He is well known for his impartial treatment of the subject for he always keeps to the **record**.

RECOURSE

Have **recourse** to: To seek the help of.

It was for existence that he was forced to have **recourse** to so many devices not sanctioned by society.

RED

Red rag to a bull: Something that excites.

He disliked a particular picture in the house so much that the sight of one served as a **red** rag to a bull.

Red letter day: An auspicious day.

15th August is the **red** letter day for every Indian.

Red tape: Official formality.

Quick work is impossible where there is **red** tapism.

REDUCE

Reduce to: Changed into.

He was **reduced** to a skeleton owing to prolonged sickness.

REED

Broken **reed**: Unreliable person.

He is broken **reed** for he has twice betrayed me.

To lean in a **reed**: To trust (or depend on) a weak person or a thing.

You are only leaning on a **reed** if you trust in the fitness of this car.

REEF

To take in a **reef**: To move cautiously.

Diplomats usually take in a **reef** while discussing important things.

REEK

Amid **reek** and squalor: Fetid atmosphere.

The refugees live amid **reek** and squalor.

REEL

Reel off: To say something rapidly.

The beggar **reeled** off a very nice story of his childhood.

Off the **reel**: In rapid succession.

It is difficult for us to keep pace with the events taking place off the **reel** in China.

REFLECT

To **reflect** upon: To ponder over.
> It is a matter worthy to **reflect** upon.

REFUGE

Take **refuge** in: To take shelter.
> The fugitives took **refuge** in the near by bung.

REGARD

With **regard** to: As regards.
> I have some suggestion to make with **regard** to your schemes.

In this **regard**: In this respect.
> I remember having warned him in this **regard**.

REIN

Give **reins** to: To allow full freedom.
> When excited he gives **reins** to his inner feelings.

Take the **reins**: To control.
> After the successful coup, the military general took the **reins** of the government.

RELATE

In **relation** to: With reference to.
> I would like to add a few more points in **relation** to what he has just said.

Strained **relations**: Unpleasant relation.
> After that unpleasant incident their **relations** are strained.

REMONSTRATE

To **remonstrate** against: To protest.

Everybody seems to be **remonstrating** against corruption in our country.

REPARTEE

A storehouse of **repartee**: A person capable of making witty remarks.

Johnson was a storehouse of **repartee**.

RESCUE

Come to the **rescue**: To save from danger.

When we were in trouble our next door neighbor came to our **rescue**.

RESORT

A last **resort**: To take a measure when all other measures fail.

If they refuse to amicably settle the existing differences, our last **resort** will probably be war.

To **resort** to: To turn to for aid.

You should never **resort** to lying to serve your own selfish ends.

RESPECT

Pay one's **respect** to: To esteem.

I just dropped in to pay my **respect** to the old man.

RETREAT

Beat a **retreat**: To move backward.

The enemies soon beat a **retreat** when they were put under heavy fire.

RIDE

Ride rough-shod over: To be inconsiderate.

A good ruler never tries to **ride** rough-shod over his subject.

Ride for a fall: To behave recklessly.

He spent his father's money so carelessly that everyone knew he was **riding** for a fail.

RIFT

Rift in the lute: A small defeat capable of destroying the whole.

Some **rift** has taken place in the lute of his handling the foreign affairs.

RIGHT

Right and left: On both sides, in all directions.

He tried to be cheeky and I slapped him **right** and left.

Serve him **right**: To treat one as one deserves.

By degrading him the general served one of his soldiers **right**.

A step in the **right** direction: An appropriate step.

The Govt's decision to make the primary education free is surely a step in the **right** direction.

Set **right**: To correct.

My house is all in shambles and I must set it **right**.

RING

Ring in one's ears: To continue to sound in one's ears.
He was a nice singer and his voice still **rings** in
our ears.

RIOT

To run **riot**: Unrestrained revelry.
Many people run **riot** during Puja time.

RIP

To **rip** open old sores: To revive an old quarrel.
Let us not **rip** open old sores; it does not pay us.

RISE

Rise to one's feet: To stand up.
The audience **rose** to their feet as the bishop
appeared on the stage.

Rise to the occasion: To show one's ability at an
opportune time.
He can **rise** to the occasion even though he does
not show off.

RISK

Run a **risk**: To incur loss; to risk.
He ran the **risk** of losing his own life while trying to
save him from fire.

ROB

Rob one of: To deprive one of.
He has been **robbed** of his freedom.

ROLAND

Give a **Roland** for an Oliver: To give appropriate.
   It pleased him immensely as he gave his rival a
   Roland for an Oliver.

ROOST

Come home to **roost**: To recoil upon the doer.
   Curses often come home to **roost**.

ROOT

To **root** out: To uproot, to eradicate.
   It is difficult to **root** out superstition by laws.

Strike at the **root** of all evil: To cure.
   Hoarding is an anti-social activity and now the
   Government is trying to strike at the **root** of this evil.

ROSE

Under the rose: Secretly.
   He continued to help the terrorist **under** the rose.

ROUGH

Rough and ready: Unpolished but prompt.
   I can get it done by him in no time because he is
   rough and ready.

Roughs and smooths: Ups and downs.
   One must put up with the **roughs** and smooths
   of life.

RULE

Rule out: To exclude.
> The possibility of our Government's severing ties with some countries is not **ruled** out.

Rule the roots: To govern.
> It is the dictator who **rules** the roost in a socialist state.

RUN

To **run** counter: To go against.
> His ideas always **run** counter to mine.

Run one's eyes over: To give a cursory glance.
> I **ran** my eyes over yesterday's Newspaper.

Run short: Insufficient.
> I am **running** short of my purse.

In the long **run**: Eventually.
> He is sure to shine in the long **run**.

S

SACK

Give (Get) the **sack**: To discharge or to be discharged.
    The manager gave his secretary the **sack**.

SAD

In **sad** earnest: Seriously.
    As he wanted his parents to understand his
    viewpoint, he related the story in **sad** earnest.

Sad dog: Scapegoat.
    A desperate man sometimes make himself a **sad**
    dog under trying circumstances.

SADDLE

In the **saddle**: In power.
    So long as he is in the **saddle** he will never allow
    any rowdy elements to get the upperhand.

Saddled with: To be burdened with.
    He could not make up his mind for he was **saddled**
    with heavy debts.

To put the **saddle** on the wrong horse: To blame the
wrong person.
    In laying the balm on your brother you are outing
    the **saddle** on the wrong horse.

SAFE

Safe and sound: In good condition.
He was glad to know that his children had arrived **safe** and sound.

Sail close to the wind: To go against a law.
He **sailed** close to the wind unnoticed in the past but ultimately be fell into his own trap.

Sail under false colours: To perform the role of a hypocrite.
It pricks the conscience of decent man to **sail** under false colours.

Sail in the same boat: To be equally exposed to danger or risk.
You can join him in his venture if you want to **sail** in the same boat.

SALAD

Salad days: Youthful experience.
When we indulge in fun and frolick the older people are reminded of their **salad** days.

SAKE

For goodness's **sake**: For the sake (honour) of goodness.
For goodness' **sake**, please do that.

SALT

Eat one's **salt**: To be a guest or a dependent.
You have been eaten his **salt** and you can never betray him.

<u>Take with a grain of **salt**</u>: To consider something cautiously.

His story does not seem very true and it must be taken with a grain of **salt**.

<u>Worth his **salt**</u>: Efficient; great man.

I cannot keep him any longer for he is not worth his **salt**.

SAP

<u>To **sap** one's strength</u>: To weaken.

He **sapped** his strength by working till late hours his salt.

SAUCE

<u>To serve the same **sauce**</u>: To retaliate.

It was for insolence that he wanted to serve him with the same **sauce**.

<u>Without the **sauce** of</u>: Something that makes anything lively.

Life loses much of its flavour and glamour without the **sauce** of difficulties.

SAVE

<u>**Save** the situation</u>: To prevent something from taking a worst turn.

His wise action on the spur of the moment **saved** the situation.

<u>**Save** one's face</u>: To avoid humiliation.

He did everything when he was in a fit of fury and now he finds it difficult to **save** his face.

SAY

<u>Say grace</u>: A short prayer before the meal.

He suggested that all should **say** the grace.

Have one's say: To say what one has to say.

I have no say on the subject; do what you wish to.

SCALE

<u>On a large **scale**</u>: In an extensive scale.

He has started his business on a large **scale**.

<u>Hold the **scales** even</u>: To be impartial.

A good judge always holds the **scales** even.

SCAPEGOAT

<u>To be made a **scapegoat**</u>: To be made to suffer for another's faults.

I have been made a **scapegoat** for no fault of mine.

SCATTER

<u>**Scatter** to the wind</u>: To destroy.

The floods have **scattered** the prospects of a bumper crop to the wind.

SCENT

<u>Put one on the wrong **scent**</u>: To misdirect.

There is no dearth of people in big cities who often try to put foreign travellers on the wrong **scent**.

SCOFF

<u>**Scoff** at</u>: To mock.

All the members of the committee **scoffed** at his impracticable suggestions.

SCORE

<u>Go off at **score**</u>: To start vigorously.

When occasion arises he would speak, going off at **score** in his own peculiar manner.

<u>On the **score** of</u>: On the ground of.

He was expelled from the college on the **score** of misbehaviour.

SCREW

<u>Put the **screw** on</u>: To bring pressure on.

The son put the **screw** on his father for his pocket money.

SEA

<u>Put to **sea**</u>: To set sail.

When the storms subsided he put to **sea** again.

SEAL

<u>**Seal** one's lips</u>: To keep close secret.

You need not be afraid of him, because I have **sealed** his lips.

<u>Under the **seal** of</u>: With full assurance of.

The news of his death was kept under the **seal** of silence.

SECRET

<u>Make no **secret** of</u>: Not to conceal.

He was so confident of success that he made no **secret** of his plan to take his enemy by surprise.

Take one into a **secret**: To take one into confidence.
  He took his friend into the **secret** of his success.

SEE

See one off: To see one depart.
  I went to **see** my friend off.

See the world: To gain experience.
  You must **see** the world which is outside the four
  walls of your class-room.

See through: To understand properly.
  The psychiatrists try to **see** through the unconscious
  mind of persons who are mentally deranged.

See the light: To be born.
  John **saw** the light on March 3, 1965.

SEEK

Far the **seek**: Difficult to find out.
  The reasons of his failure are not far to **seek**.

SENSE

In one **sense**: From one point of view.
  In one **sense** his statement sounds quite logical.

Frighten one out of one's **senses** (of wits): To terrify.
  The sudden explosion frightened him out of
  his **sense**.

SERPENT

Cherish a **serpent** into one's bosom: To show kindness to a person who is ungrateful.

> I should not have cherished such a **serpent** into mu bosom.

SERVE

Serve the devil: To be mischievous.

> Unfortunately today there are more people who are desirous of **serving** the devil instead of serving the lowly and the lost.

SET

Set aside: To reject.

> He **set** aside their demands for want of sufficient funds.

Set at defiance: To violate.

> A good citizen will not **set** the law of the country at defiance.

Set at naught: To despise.

> You can't, by a mere stroke of pen, **set** at naught the experience of our forefathers.

Set out: To depart.

> They have just **set** out for an evening walk.

Set on: To instigate.

> He **set** his dog on me when I walked past his house.

Set one's face against: To oppose.
> Many leaders **set** their faces against the step of the Government which sought to make regional language as the medium of instruction.

Set the Thames on fire: To do some extraordinary thing.
> Since he is a renowned scientist, his discovery will surely **set** the Thames on fire.

Set up: (1) To establish, (2) To put in power.
> (1) They have **set** up a library in their village.
> (2) They **set** up a new candidate in place of an older manager who had retrieved.

SHADE

Cast into the **shade**: To render less attractive, outshine.
> He cast the fame of his brother into the **shade**.

Shadow of a **shade**: Absolutely nothing.
> The government becomes a mere shadow of a **shade** when the people succeed in taking law into their hands.

No **shadow** of doubt: No doubt.
> There is no **shadow** of doubt that the country is passing through a very critical period.

SHELF

On the **shelf**: Put aside.
> His application for increment has been on the **shelf** for want of sufficient funds.

SHOE

To step into another person's **shoe**: To take another's place.

India has not produced anyone to step into the **shoes** of Gandhiji.

SHOOT

Shooting pain: Acute pain.

He is having a **shooting** headache.

Shoot Niagara: Desperate enterprise.

This task of ours is going to be something like **shooting** Niagara.

SHOP

To talk **shop**: To talk about one's own business.

People do not relish his habit of always talking **shop** to them.

SHORT

Be **short** of: Be less than.

His performance in the last **sports** fell short the marks.

SHOULDER

To **shoulder** responsibility: To take a responsibility.

It is too risky a job and he is ready to **shoulder** the responsibility.

Rub **shoulders** with: To be intimate with.

He made his fortune by rubbing his **shoulders** with some big people.

Have a head on one's **shoulder**: To possess ability.
Nehru definitely had his head on his **shoulder** else, he would not have been able to steer the country clear of so many political crises.

Put one's **shoulders** to the wheel: To exert.
You have my blessings but you must put your **shoulder** to the wheel.

SIDE

Side by side: Along with.
Christianity and Hinduism are two religions which are flourishing **side** by side in India.

SIGHT

Lose **sight** of: Overlook.
In this world of shifting values the importance of character is often lost **sight** of.

Cannot bear the **sight**: Not to be able to endure.
He cannot bear the **sight** of any strong and stout man begging in the street.

SILENCE

Silent as grave: Very quiet.
When the commander appeared at the scene, the soldiers were as **silent** as the grave.

SINEWS

Sinews of war: That which gives strength.
Man-power, money and agricultural output can be considered as the **sinews** of war.

SINK

Sink or swim: Do or die; fail or succeed.

> I cannot afford to give you more; either you **sink** or swim.

SKATE

Skate on thin ice: To handle a risky affair.

> He is intelligent and fearless and he loves to **skate** on thin ice.

SKELETON

Skeleton in the cupboard: Some domestic source of trouble.

> It is because of your carelessness the **skeleton** in your cupboard will get worse day by day.

SKIN

Escape with the **skin** of one's teeth: To escape narrowly.

> The two boys of our college escaped with the **skin** of their teeth in the riot yesterday.

Save one's **skin**: To escape safely.

> We try to save our own **skin** in times of distress.

Thick **skinned**: Not perturbed by criticism.

> He being a thick **skinned** man seldom takes any notice of public criticism very seriously.

SKIP

Skip over: To omit.

> The professor told her to **skip** over a paragraph in reading.

SKY

<u>**Sky** is the limit</u>: There is no limit.
No one can hazard a guess as to where the researches of space scientists may led because **sky** is limit for them.

SLEEP

<u>**Sleep** like a log</u>: Sleep soundly.
He **slept** like a log.

<u>**Sleep** over a question</u>: Leave it to the next day.
This being a very difficult question, you can ill-afford to **sleep** over it.

SLIP

<u>Give the **slip**</u>: To elude.
He was clever enough to give us the **slip** yesterday.

<u>A **slip** of pen (or tongue)</u>: An unintentional mistake made in writing or speaking.
It was a mere **slip** of tongue (or pen) so you must not attach undue importance to it.

<u>**Slip** through one's fingers</u>: To escape from one's grasp.
I will not let the opportunity **slip** through my fingers.

SLEEVE

<u>To roll up one's **sleeve**</u>: To get ready to fight.
He was furious and he started rolling up his **sleeves**.

SMILE

<u>Wear a **smile**</u>: To present joyous appearance.

The entire town wore a **smile** at the time of the Prime minister's visit.

<u>Wreathed in **smiles**</u>: To look happy.

Bonita's face was wreathed in **smiles** when she saw her husband back from the battlefield.

SNAP

To **snap** at: To talk sharply.

You should stop **snapping** at him like that.

SOUR

Sour one's temper: To make one's temper harsh.

It is the way he behaves that **sours** his master's temper.

SPEAK

To **speak** of one is high terms: To praise.

The principal **spoke** of him in high terms.

Speak well for: Favourable indication of.

His straight forwardness in speech and tidiness in his dress **spoke** well for him.

SPELL

<u>Under one's **spell**</u>: To be fascinated.

He could not but fall under her spell.

<u>Cast a **spell**</u>: To enchant.

His speech cast a **spell** on the public mind.

SPIN

Spin a yarn: To tell tales.
  The old man was good at **spinning** yarns.

SQUARE

Square with: To agree with.
  His statement does not **square** with mine.

Speak on the **square**: To speak honestly.
  He did not have audacity to speak on the **square**.

Square one's accounts: To settle one's accounts.
  I am thinking of **squaring** my accounts with you
  before it is too late.

STAND

Stand one in good stead: To be of great advantage.
  The old man handed over a packet to his son and
  said, "Keep it nicely and it will **stand** you in good
  stead some day.

Stand in the way of: To obstruct.
  You **stand** in the way of my success.

Stand it (out): To face bravely.
  I will **stand** the challenge out.

Stand the test: To emerge out successful in the test.
  I will **stand** by my previous commitment if your love
  stands the acid test of time.

STEM

Stem the tide: To resist.

He had to **stem** the tide of his rivals, to enjoy the loaves and fishes of politics.

STILL

Still water runs deep: Unassuming person have commonly great abilities.

There is no doubt about his wonderful achievement. **Still** water runs deep.

STIR

To **stir** up: To excite.

The communists tried to **stir** up new troubles in our town.

STONE

To leave no **stone** unturned: To spare no pains in order to obtain an object.

He left no **stone** unturned in achieving his goal.

Within a **stone's** throw: A very short distance.

His house is within a **stone's** throw from my place.

SWEAT

By the **sweat** one's brow: By hard labour.

The peasants in our country earn their living by the **sweat** of their brow.

SWIM

Swim with the stream: To follow the people in general. People who lack courage to oppose **swim** with stream of public opinion.

SWING

In full **swing**: In full motion.
The construction work in our college is in full **swing**.

T

TABLE

To turn the **tables**: To reverse the conditions.
    When the new minister came to power everyone
    thought that the tables would be turned.

TAKE

Taken aback: To be surprised.
    We were **taken** aback by his rude answers.

Take after: To resemble.
    She **takes** after her mother.

Take in good part: To accept in a friendly spirit.
    His words are too sharp to be **taken** in good part.

To **take** one by surprise: To come upon one
unexpectedly.
    The police **took** the robbers by surprise and
    unearthed a good deal of stolen property.

To **take** for: To mistake for.
    I **mistook** an ordinary piece of shining glass for a
    diamond.

Take one a task: To rebuke.
    The manager **took** one of his workers to task for
    lack of interest in his work.

Take up with: To show a liking for; to fall in love with.
He was **taken** up with a girl who was more immature mentally.

TAMPER

Tamper with: Meddle with.
Somebody has definitely tried to **tamper** with my letter.

TANGENT

To go (Fly) off at a **tangent**: To suddenly go to a different direction while discussing a certain point.
Smith often flies off at a **tangent**.

TASTE

To one's **taste**: To one's liking.
Playing bridge is not to my **taste**.

TAX

Tax the brain: To make heavy demand.
One has to **tax** the brain during the examination.

TEARS

Bathe in **tears**: To burst into tears.
Her eyes bathed in **tears** when she was reunited with her family after many years.

TEETH

In the **teeth** of: In opposition of.
The language bill was passed in the **teeth** of much resistance from the opposition members.

Show one's **teeth**: To threaten.
> The wounded tiger showed its **teeth** to the hunter to retaliate.

Tooth and nail: By all possible means.
> They fought **tooth** and nail to regain their lost glory.

TELL

Tell upon: To affect.
> Remember, worries will surely **tell** upon your health.

Tell one's beads: To count beads while offering a prayer.
> The lamas in the monasteries **tell** their beads while chanting hymns.

TERM

Be on **terms** with: To be on friendly relations with.
> Rajesh and Shaid are not on **terms** with each other.

Bring to **terms**: To force to accept conditions.
> He brought the two rival parties to **terms**.

Come to **terms**: To come to an agreement.
> The mediator can make some substantial progress if the two parties show their willingness to come to **terms**.

TETHER

At the end of one's **tether**: To be at the end of one's strength.
> You must go with him till the end of your **tether**.

THICK

As **thick** as thieves: Very friendly.
>Chester is as **thick** as thieves with Ross.

Through **thick** and thin: Under all circumstances.
>He pursued his policy through **thick** and thin.
>Nehru had some **thick** and thin supporters.

In the **thick** of: In the midst of.
>He never lost his self respect even though he was in the **thick** of trying circumstances.

THREAD

Thread one's way through: To pass through a narrow way.
>I had to **thread** my way through the crowd to see you.

THRESHOLD

On the **threshold** of: On the point of beginning.
>The chancellor told the engineer graduates that they now stand on the **threshold** of a new life.

THROAT

Thrust a thing down one's **throat**: To force one to accept.
>I could not possibly think of anything because I was in the **throes** of a very important examination.

THROUGH

Through and through: completely.
>That he is **through** and through an aristocrat is known to all.

THROW

Throw light on: To make clear.

This article **throws** much light on the shape of things to come.

Throw off the scent: To led astray.

He tried to **throw** me off the scent when I wanted to know the secrets.

THUMB

Under one's **thumb**: Under one's influence.

His child refused to live, under the **thumb** of his uncle any longer.

THUNDER

To steal one's **thunder**: To snatch glory from.

Can anyone steal the **thunder** of our beloved leader?

TIME

Time and again: Frequently.

He has been warned **time** and again not to indulge in smoking.

Have a fine **time**: To enjoy.

He had a fine **time** at home during the holidays.

From time to **time**: At certain intervals.

He went to see his ailing brother from **time** to time.

In no **time**: Quickly.

I can finish this work in no **time**.

At **times**: Occasionally.
>He gets mentally upset at **times**.

TIP

On the **tip** of one's tongue: Just about to say.
>He entered into my room furiously with an
>expression of indignation on the **tip** of his tongue.

On **tiptoe**: Silently.
>She went on **tiptoe** to the door and put the latch on.

TOE

Toe the line: To do as others.
>The new chief minister simply **toed** of your
>neighbours.

Tread on one's **toes**: To hurt the feelings of.
>It does not pay to tread on the **toes** of your
>neighbours.

TOIL

Toil and moil: To labour hard.
>The poor man had to **toil** and moil all through for
>the sake of his family.

TOM

Tom, Dick and Harry: Ordinary people.
>You can't expect any **Tom**, Dick and Harry to do this
>difficult job.

TONGUE

To have a long **tongue**: Talkative.
>Most of the girls in her class have long **tongues**.

<u>Have one's **tongue** tied</u>: Not able to speak freely.
Being a subordinate officer his **tongue** is tied.

<u>Hold one's **tongue**</u>: To keep silent.
When the elders speak the children should hold their **tongues**.

<u>To speak with one's **tongue** in one's cheek</u>: To speak ironically.
One should not take his words seriously because he usually speaks with his **tongue** in his cheeks.

<u>To keep one's **tongue** still</u>: To keep quiet.
The teacher told her pupils to keep their **tongues** still.

TOUCH

<u>**Touch** on</u>: Mention briefly.
The professor **touched** briefly on the failures of democracy in many countries in the Middle-East and South-East Asia.

<u>**Touch** on tender point</u>: To strike one in the delicate point.
This remark **touched** her on a tender point.

TRACK

<u>Beaten **track**</u>: Usual course
If we traverse the beaten **track** of history we can surely find that the basic problems of human beings have always been the same.

TRIFLE

<u>**Trifle** with</u>: Treat lightly.

The disease being a dangerous one, should not be **trifled** with.

TRUMP

<u>Hold the **trump** card</u>: To possess means which promises success.

India holds the **trump** card in Kashmir.

TUNE

<u>To be in **tune** with</u>: In agreement with.

What he says is not in **tune** with what he does.

<u>To the **tune** of</u>: To the amount of.

He has spent to the **tune** of five hundred rupees only in a couple of days.

TURN

<u>Not to **turn** a hair</u>: Not to be disturbed.

He answered all the questions without **turning** a hair.

<u>Do a good **turn**</u>: Good deed.

He has done me a good **turn**.

<u>**Turn** the tide</u>: To change the course.

Nehru's revolutionary thoughts **turned** the tide of history.

<u>Twists and **turns**</u>: Intricacies.

He finds difficulty in understanding the twists and **turns** of logic.

U

UNDER

Under-dog: The lowly and the lost.
Gandhi always fought for the **under**-dogs.

Under one's eyes (or nose): Under one's observation.
The boy cannot be mischievous because he is
always **under** the professor's eyes.

Under the sun: Anywhere in the world.
It is difficult to find a place better than Shimla **under**
the sun.

Under fire: To the fire of the enemy.
The Saigon airport was **under** enemy's fire.

UP

Up and doing: active; alert.
We must be **up** and doing to the task we are out to
achieve.

Uphill task: Hard work.
The government is faced with an **uphill** task.

UPPER-HAND

Upper-hand: Advantage.

He is trying his best to get an **upper**-hand over his colleague.

UTOPIAN

Utopian dream: Impracticable scheme.

This is an **utopian** dream which no sensible person should indulge in.

V

VAIN

In **vain**: Without effect; to no purpose.
    He fought in **vain**.

At **variance** with: Disagreement.
    His words are often at **variance** with his deeds.

VAGRANT

Vagrant speculations: Idle thoughts.
    Indulging in **vagrant** thoughts has not led you anywhere.

VAN

In the **van** of: At the head of.
    Industrious people who are at one time seen at the lowest rung of the ladder of fame, will be, at another time, seen far in the **van**.

VANISH

Vanishing point: Point of disappearance.
    The path of glory and the pomp of power-all lead to death which is the **vanishing** point of all our activities.

Vanity fair: World of folly and fashion.
    We all love to roam about in this **vanity** fair.

VEIL

To take the **veil**: To become a nun.
> She took the **veil** after her graduation from the Harvard University.

Beyond the **veil**: Life after death; another world.
> We cannot hazard a guess as to what happens beyond the **veil**.

To drop the **veil**: To cover.
> This has generated so much of ill-feeling that we must drop the **veil** over this question.

VEIN

In lighter **vein**: Humorously.
> The story was written in a lighter **vein**.

VELVET

Velvet paw: Cruelty veiled under pleasant manners.
> You should be careful with the **velvet** paw of this man.

With an iron hand in a **velvet** (glove): Outward gentleness cloaking inflexibility.
> Administrators rule the country with an iron hand in a **velvet** glove.

VENGEANCE

With a **vengeance**: Violently.
> He killed the murderer with a **vengeance**.

VENTURE

At a **venture**: At random.

>He tried many shots at a **venture** with a view to scaring his enemies.

Venture on (upon): To dare.

>It is sheer foolishness to **venture** upon such a project.

VERGE

On the **verge** of: On the brink of; very near.

>Because of famines and floods country is on the **verge** of ruin.

VERSE

Be **versed** in: Adept in.

>He is well **versed** is Sanskrit literature.

VICTIM

Fall **victim** to: To be ruined.

>He fell a **victim** to his wickedness.

VIE

Vie with: To strive for superiority.

>The farmers **vied** with each other for the prize.

VIEW

With a **view** to: For the purpose of.

>He strove hard with a **view** to improving his position in the class.

In **view** of: Having regard to.
   The boy was given full freeship in **view** of his
   position in the class.

To take a **view** of: To study.
   He took a **view** of the situation.

To come to **view**: To be seen.
   The hills came to **view** at long last.

Point of **view**: Opinion.
   I fully subscribe to your point of **view**.

VIRGIN

Virgin soil: That has never been cultivated.
   They were fortunate to find sufficient **virgin** soil in
   the newly discovered island.

VIRTUE

By **virtue** of: By dint of.
   By **virtue** of his painstaking labour he was
   successful in his examination.

VISTA

To open up a new **vista**: To show new possibilities and
prospect.
   Space researches have opened up a new **vista**.

VOGUE

In **vogue**: In practice.
   Mini-skirts are in **vogue** in many western countries.

W

WADE

Well **wadded** with: Full of.

His life is well-**wadded** with misery.

To **wade** through: To go through.

I have no time to **wade** through your lengthy document.

WAIF

Waifs and strays: Homeless persons.

The street of Kolkata is full of **waifs** and strays.

To **wait** upon: To attend as a servant.

The coolie **waited** on the lady.

To lie in **wait**: Ambush; await.

Good fortunes lie in **wait** for industrious man.

WAKE

In the **wake**: Following immediately after.

In the **wake** of floods comes famine.

On the **wane**: Declining.

His popularity is on the **wane**.

For **want** of: Lack of.

The soldiers could not fight for **want** of sufficient ammunitions.

Wanting in: Deficient.

He was never found **wanting** in genuine interest in studies.

WAR

To wage a **war**: To make war.

Waging **wars** is basically due to gross misunderstanding among nations.

Cold **war**: Hostile relations between nations.

There is a cold **war** going on between India and Pakistan.

Ward off: To drive back.

This step was taken to **ward** off possible dangers from the enemy's side.

Warp and woof: Perverse or different inclinations of mind.

Two opposite qualities are so fused that they appear like **warp** and woof of his personality.

WASH

To **wash** dirty linen in public: To speak or accuse in public of unpleasant private affairs.

No sensible man would like to **wash** his dirty linen in the public.

Wash one's hands of: To cut off all connections with.

He has **washed** his hands of whole business.

Wash out: Poor in ability.
  He being a complete **wash** out failed his
  examination.

WATER

In smooth **waters**: Without any troubles.
  The world is a difficult place to live in as we cannot
  always expect to be in smooth **waters**.

In deep **waters**: In difficulties.
  He has been in deep **waters** after the sudden
  disappearance of his brother.

Of the first **water**: Of the best quality.
  He is a poet of the first **water**.

To keep one's head above **water**: To avoid financial
worries.
  He spends his money carefully so as to keep his
  head always above **water**.

To throw cold **water** on: To dishearten.
  He tried his best to throw cold **water** on this project
  but failed miserably.

WAY

By **way** of: For the purpose of.
  He added a few lines by **way** of illustrations.

By the **way**: As we proceed on.
  By the **way**, have you been to your uncle's house?

Go a long **way**: Be of great help or importance.
   Perseverance goes a long **way** in making one's life worthy of living.

Have one's **way**: To do as one wishes.
   No matter what you say, he will have his own **way**.

One **way** or the other: Any way.
   He will be punished one **way** or the other for his mischief.

Go the **way** of the world (or flesh): To die.
   He too had gone the **way** of all the flesh.

WEAR

Wear and tear: Decay.
   The house has stood the **wear** and tear for a long time.

Wear out: To render useless by decay.
   He is so slow that it almost **wears** out my patience.

Wear on: To pass slowly.
   He never lost his faith in his final victory as the days **wore** on.

WEATHER

Weather a storm: To face difficulties bravely.
   You will be a real hero if you **weather** this storm.

WEDGE

<u>Thin end (edge) of the **wedge**</u>: An insignificant beginning leading to great and important developments.

Starting a small shop on the wayside proved to be a thin end of the **wedge**.

WHEEL

Wheels <u>within wheels</u>: Intricate machinery; a complication of circumstances.

He loves going to factories and no wonder there are **wheels** within wheels.

<u>To break a butterfly on the **wheel**</u>: To inflict punishment out of all proportions.

The manager should not have been so inconsiderate; his action was like breaking a butterfly on the **wheel**.

Wheel <u>of life</u>: Vital processes.

The **wheel** of life goes moving on and on.

WIDE

Wide <u>awake</u>: On the alert.

I was too **wide** awake to allow him to play the fool.

WILD

<u>Spread like **wild** fire</u>: To spread to all directions.

The news of Sastri's death spread like **wild** fire.

<u>**Wild** goose chase</u>: A foolish pursuit.

If you have a little bit of common sense, you will surely give up this **wild** goose chase.

WIND

Have (set) **wind** of: To get information of something about to happen.

He seems to have got the **wind** of my good fortune.

In the **wind**: About to happen.

It is in the **wind** that Russia might test its new atomic weapon in near future.

Fling to the **winds**: Abandon.

He has to filing the idea of starting this scheme to the **winds** because of the non-availability of funds.

How the **wind** blows: To try to understand the state of affairs.

He just wants to know how the **wind** blows.

To come from four **winds**: To come from all directions.

He received birthday greetings from the four **winds**.

WIPE

Wipe off: To remove by rubbing; erase.

There is a thick layer of dust on the table. Please **wipe** it off.

Wipe out: Destroy.

Nuclear wars will **wipe** human beings out of existence.

WITH

Within an ace of: Very near.

The army was **within** an ace of defeat when it obtained some reinforcement.

WOLF

<u>A **wolf** in the sheep's clothing (skin)</u>: A wicked and deceitful person.

> David spotted him at once as a **wolf** in sheep's clothing.

<u>To hold the **wolf** by the ears</u>: To be in a situation where one can neither advance not retreat, nor carry on.

> By accepting the job he has simply held the **wolf** by the ears.

WOMAN

<u>Play the **woman**</u>: Weep.

> It does not behave you to play the **woman** like this.

<u>**Woman** of the world</u>: Experienced; fashionable.

> She is a **woman** of the world.

WOOD

<u>Cannot see the **wood** for the trees</u>: Details obstruct general view.

> Overburdened with flies, the so called social worker failed to see the **wood** for the trees.

<u>Out for **wood**</u>: Out of or free from troubles.

> So long as he is there I am never out of the **wood**.

WORTH

<u>**Worth** one's while</u>: Advantageous.

> It is not **worth** his while to involve himself in such a hearted argument with him.

<u>WRECK</u>

Wreck <u>and ruin</u>: Destruction.

The industries of the country are going to **wreck** and ruin because of gheraoes and strikes.

<u>WRITE</u>

Write <u>a good hand</u>: Skilled in the use of pen.

The boy **writes** a very good hand.

Write <u>off</u>: Cencel.

We have to **write** off all his dues.

<u>WRONG</u>

Wrong <u>side of thirty</u>: Exceeding thirty years of age.

He is on the **wrong** side of thirty.

Y

YEAR

Year in and year out: Continuously.

He has been doing the same old job **year** in and year out.

Year after year: Year by year.

The boy was making a tremendous progress year after **year**.

All the **year** round: Throughout the year.

He never showed any sign of slackness all the **year** round.

Year of discretion: An age when one is capable of distinguishing between right and wrong.

YEOMAN

Yeoman service: Valuable service.

The **yeoman** service rendered by the Gurkhas in the field of defence has been acclaimed by many.

YOKE

Throw off the **yoke** of: To be free from the control of.

Inspired by the patriotic writings of Nehru and Gandhi, many Asian threw off the **yoke** of their rulers.

Z

ZEAL

Zest and **zeal**: With great interest.
   One should do one's work with zest and **zeal**.

To be at one's **zenith**: To be at the pinnacle of.
   Nehru was at his **zenith** of his glory when he
   breathed his last a few years ago.

To add **zest** to: To make more lively.
   Difficulties add **zest** to life.